VOICE - OVER VOICE ACTOR

WHAT IT'S LIKE BEHIND THE MIC

YURI LOWENTHAL AND TARA PLATT

Voice-Over Voice Actor: What It's Like Behind the Mic
by Yuri Lowenthal and Tara Platt

Bug Bot Press
1335 N. La Brea #2233
Hollywood, CA 90028
orders@bugbotpress.com; http://wwwBugBotPress.com

Unattributed quotations are by Yuri Lowenthal and Tara Platt

Edition ISBNs
ISBN 13: 978-0-9840740-0-6
ISBN 10: 0-9840740-0-7

Cover design, layout and typesetting by Cyanotype Book Architects
Illustrations by Jerzy Drozd. Photographs by Boris Kievsky.

Printed in the United States of America
Printed on recycled paper.

Library of Congress Cataloging-in-Publication Data

Lowenthal, Yuri.
Voice-over voice actor : what it's like behind the
mic / by Yuri Lowenthal and Tara Platt. -- 1st ed.
p. cm.
Includes bibliographical references and index.
LCCN 2009931112
ISBN-13: 978-0-9840740-0-6
ISBN-10: 0-9840740-0-7

1. Voice-overs. 2. Voice-overs--Vocational guidance.
3. Voice actors and actresses.   I. Platt, Tara.
II. Title.

PN1995.9.V63L69 2009   791.4'023
                              QBI09-600111

WHAT OTHERS ARE SAYING ABOUT
Voice-Over Voice Actor: What It's Like Behind the Mic

"As professionals, we attempt to recognize talent and integrity. Yuri and Tara are heads and shoulders ahead of their contemporaries. Their combined integrity and work ethic, along with a strong acting aptitude, keep them on their own personal and joyous track for success."

• HARVEY & CATHY KALMENSON,
KALMENSON & KALMENSON, INC., VOICE CASTING & INSTRUCTION

"In my eight years of coaching actors of all levels, I have never seen such a comprehensive and clear explanation of the ins and outs of the voice industry. Yuri and Tara offer up a book that is not only easy to follow, it's also in-depth, inspiring, and funny at the same time!"

• DALLAS TRAVERS, FOUNDER OF
THE THRIVING ARTIST CIRCLE & AUTHOR OF THE TAO OF SHOW BUSINESS

"Lowenthal and Platt delve deep into the world of voice acting, with stories from behind the mic and trenchant observations from fellow performers. They bust the jargon-packed world of loop groups and walla work, voice matching and phone patching. They have produced an excellent road map of the surprisingly wide world of vocal performance, including unexpected areas like studio socializing, the ethics of networking, audition tips, and even health and hydration. The result is an invaluable guide to professional voice acting, from two of its leading stars."

• JONATHAN CLEMENTS, AUTHOR,
SCHOOLGIRL MILKY CRISIS: ADVENTURES IN THE ANIME AND MANGA TRADE

"Whatever Yuri and Tara say, I wholeheartedly disagree with. They're a couple of shysters. And if you believe that, then I am Elmer J. Fudd, millionaire. I own a mansion and a yacht. Buy this book, you maroons!"

• JOHN DiMAGGIO, ACTOR,
FUTURAMA, GEARS OF WAR, HALO 3

TABLE OF CONTENTS

ACKNOWLEDGEMENTS

This book would never have been possible without the generous help of our fellow VAs, our friends, our families, and most of all our fans. And here's to those who really got their hands dirty: Jennifer, Juan, Stephanie, Candace, and Jonathan, who read what we had written and gave their honest opinions so that we might bring you, the reader, the best possible book. Tod and the gang at Thomson-Shore, you helped demystify and yet romanticize the process of actually printing a physical book. To our fantastic design team Scott and Sarah at Cyanotype, for making things, well, *look* so darned good. To Casey and Rudy for making us look cool on the intarwebs. To Boris for so much more than the pretty photos you took of us. To Jerzy for finally turning us into what we've always wanted to be: cartoons. To Paul for writing a kick-ass foreword. To SomeAudioGuy for taking us to technology school. To Dallas for lending guidance and support. To Wil for being a trailblazer whose path we could trust. To Dr. Bear for making a last-minute house call on the book. To our amazing and immaculate editor, Candace, for catching all our little oopsies but not messin' with our style. So thank you. Thank you to the wonderful team of people who actually made this book possible.

DEDICATION

This book is dedicated to our parents Barry, Candace, Heidi, and Jim, who have always supported our crazy ideas and relentless pursuit of our dreams.

This book is dedicated to the ridiculously talented voice-over community, whose members rarely get the acknowledgement they deserve.

This book is dedicated to the fans, who make it possible for us to do what we do.

This book is dedicated to anyone who has passion, a dream, and the drive to succeed.

This book is dedicated to you.

Disclaimer, AKA "What Exactly Are You Promising Here?"

First, what our lawyer told us to say:

This book is designed to provide information on voice-over, voice acting, self-promotion, vocal health, and warm-ups. It is sold with the understanding that the publisher and authors (and guest experts) are not engaged in rendering legal, medical, or other professional services. If legal, medical, or other expert assistance is required, the services of a competent professional should be sought. There are physical exercises described in this book; we do not recommend engaging in any type of new physical activity without first consulting a physician.

It is also not the aim of this book to imply that there is only way to build a voice-over career; nor is there a guarantee that by reading this book, you will have a successful career in the world of voice-over.

Voice-over is not a get-rich-quick endeavor. Anyone who decides to pursue a career in the entertainment business must expect to invest a lot of time, energy, and very likely, money, into it. For many people we know, voice-over is an exciting, rewarding career, and a lot of them have built solid names for themselves in this business.

Every effort has been made to make this book as complete and accurate as possible. However, there may be mistakes, both typographical and in content. Therefore, this book should be used as a guide and not the ultimate source in voice-over, voice acting, the care of your voice, and related subjects that we touch on.

The purpose of this book is to educate and entertain. The authors and Bug Bot Press shall have neither liability nor responsibility to any person or entity with respect to loss or damage caused, or alleged to have been caused, directly or indirectly, by the information contained in this book.

If you do not wish to be bound by the above, you may return this book to the publisher for a full refund.

And in our own words:

We're going to try to answer a couple of questions you may have while flipping through this book, contemplating its purchase:

"If I read this book, will I become a famous voice actor?"

Maybe. Certainly not just because you read this book. It's going to take a lot more than reading this book (or any other, for that matter) for you to become famous. The *only* thing we can guarantee is that by reading this book you'll be more well-read and slightly older. But here's the deal: we've geared this book towards your having fun, learning stuff, and getting excited about voice acting; not towards your getting famous. This type of work has no guarantee, no *A+B=C* plan. But it *sure* can be a lot of fun, and the people we've seen succeed have never forgotten that. If you try this stuff, and after a while you're not having fun anymore, find something that you *do* have fun doing. You'll be happier for it. Trust us: fun is way cooler than fame.

"Will everything you say in this book work for me?"

Probably not. Everybody's different. If everything worked the same for everyone, there'd be no surprises. Did the stuff we talk about in this book work for *us*? Yep. And that's what you wanted to find out, right? How we do what we do? What have we seen? Well, that's what we intend to give you ... and then some.

FOREWORD

So you want to be a voice actor? Close your eyes for a moment and listen.

All of those noises you hear – the murmurs and whispers, dripping taps and distant engine rumbles – are waves on the ocean of sound we swim through each day. Our emotions respond most viscerally to what we hear. Our lives are constantly awash with sound, though we rarely acknowledge it.

Sound is everything. If you don't believe me watch a movie minus the post-production sound design. You'll get a new appreciation for sound engineers, sound designers, and musicians. The visuals may draw us in but it's the sound that keeps us in. I believe this is why we hang on every word uttered by that chap who voices over movie trailers, and why we are equally compelled to go and beat up a mime.

Professional voice actors understand the importance of conveying information using sound. They're among the most underappreciated and they're among the most talented. Consider that a film or television actor can convey emotion or meaning with a raised eyebrow or a nuanced expression. Voice actors enjoy no such advantage. If it can't be done with just the voice, then it can't be done.

If you haven't run screaming thus far – and assuming you've opened your eyes and read down to here – don't fret; because you've come to the right place. Tara Platt and Yuri Lowenthal are among the best at what they do, and they're here to guide you gently and whimsically through the pieces you'll need to know. *Voice-Over Voice Actor* is the essential handbook, specifically geared towards what really happens when you do this for a living. You'll read this book over and over again.

In addition to being accomplished and talented voice actors, Tara and Yuri are two of the sweetest and funniest people I know. That sense of fun jumps from these pages and will put you at ease now that I've frightened the life out of you. If we are all afloat on this ocean of sound, they're piloting the lifeboat.

Let's go test the water.

PAUL JENKINS
Atlanta, June 2009

Paul Jenkins is an Eisner Award-winning author and comic book creator. Some of his many stand-outs include The Sentry, The Spectacular Spider-Man, Wolverine: Origin, *and* Captain America. *In addition to his prolific comic works, he has written and directed numerous voice-overs for video games, including his own award-winning hit game* The Darkness.

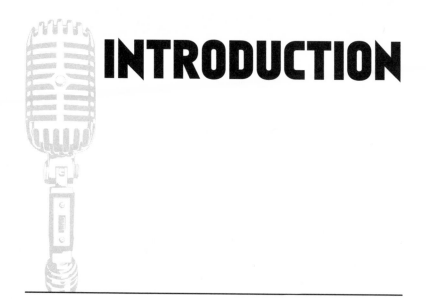

INTRODUCTION

---

*"The supreme accomplishment is to blur the line
between work and play."*

ARNOLD TOYNBEE, ENGLISH ECONOMIC HISTORIAN

WHY WE WROTE THIS BOOK

It certainly wasn't our intention to write a book when we started out in this crazy business. All we wanted to do was make a buck doing something we love, and that thing was acting. So we acted.

First, we acted before we even knew we could make any money at it. We were the self-styled hams at family gatherings, the class clown in elementary school, Juliet on a high school stage, comedians in cafes and clubs, a thousand-and-one characters (and most of the crew) in summer stock theatre. We made our own Super 8 films (what the kids today are calling "videos") and bared our souls (and on occasion, more than that) in dark basement theaters off-off-*off* Broadway, where often there were more of us on stage than in the seats. It wasn't always easy, but something kept us going.

Then miraculously, a time came when somebody paid us for our acting. Now it may not have covered even our bus fare to the theater, but it didn't matter. We weren't doing it for money. But the thought arose: *I've already made this my life. Could I actually make a living at it?* We started reading the papers, looking at billboards, watching TV. We could see the people who were making a living doing what we love. The *stars*. If they could do it, why couldn't we? So we set out to be the next overnight success (forgetting, for a moment, that we'd already been doing this for years).

And it was hard again. Most people didn't want to pay us, and those who did, couldn't pay us what we needed to survive. But survive we did. We took other jobs that had nothing to do with acting (unless acting like you really wanted to be there counts), and that allowed us to do more acting. And more ... and more. We took classes, auditioned for anyone who'd let us in the door, worked on student films, assisted famous directors, wrangled pigs for eccentric Japanese performers. (These are, of course, stories for another book). We lived our lives, and every odd little experience helped prepare us for the next acting job.

Then it started to happen. We found that what we practiced for every day, what we trained for, sweated and bled for, is what we were starting to become. We were actors. People started paying us a little more regularly ... for things that had started out as fun and games, mind you.

Even then, it was still a surprise when we stumbled into voice acting. I mean, we'd watched cartoons for years (one of us a little more than the other), and we still had memories of their callouts:

GO, SPEED RACER!

AUTOBOTS, ROLL OUT!

AND KNOWING IS HALF THE BATTLE!

S.I.G. SIGNAL IS GREEN!

WHEN CAPTAIN AMERICA THROWS HIS MIGHTY SHIELD ...

SWORD OF OMENS, GIVE ME SIGHT BEYOND SIGHT!

MEANWHILE, BACK AT THE HALL OF JUSTICE ...

But that's not a *real* job, is it? Is it? *Hmm. I don't know. Let's take a voice acting class and find out.*

So we did. We went to class. We recorded voice-over demos. We sent them to agents. And it finally started to click. We started to work. We learned more. And, astoundingly enough, we even started to get paid for our voice acting. On a regular basis, no less! Soon, we were making enough money so that we didn't have to work as secretaries and bartenders anymore. We were working on projects we could write home to our families about, and that they could watch on their TVs at home in Michigan and Tennessee.

It was an interesting time. And an interesting thing happened: we started to get letters. (Okay, well, *e-mails*, mostly.) They were from people we didn't know. People from the U.S., people from the U.K., people from Canada and France and the Philippines and Dubai and New Zealand. And they wanted to know how they, too, could do what we were doing: "How did you get to where you are?"

Hold on; wait! We *did* know those people. They were us. We remembered that not so long ago, we, too, wrote letters to people we looked up to, asking for encouragement and advice.

We stood in line for hours at sci-fi and comic book conventions (okay, once again, one of us more than the other) for a chance to ask those people, our heroes, how we could do what they were doing.

The more e-mails we got asking us those same questions, the more it became important to write this book. Through love, relentlessness, and a little luck, we had gotten to a place other people wanted to get to as well. How could we not share the fantastical world we live in?

Actors have a pretty cool job. We get to try on different ... people. We get to create characters that have unique mannerisms or personality quirks that we ourselves might not actually share. For on-camera actors, these characters are limited only by the actor's imagination and appearance. Imagine how often you see an on-camera actor in an interview and realize that he or she isn't what you had imagined based on the characters the actor plays.

Now take that one step further: as voice actors, we aren't constrained by age, gender, race, or even *species*. If we can create a voice for a character, we can play that character!

Voice-over is an amazingly empowering medium for any actor with an imagination and an inclination to play. There's no age, sex, or race discrimination (okay, there's never *none* of that stuff, but you will find less of it around here). Why keep it a secret?

We wish someone had told us some of this stuff sooner, so now we're taking it on ourselves to share the information with others.

So here you go. We're throwing you a rope. It may not get you all the way here, and you're gonna have to grab it yourself, but it'll be an exciting climb if you decide to make it. That we can promise.

AND WHO ARE WE ANYWAY?

Well, for now we'll tell you that Yuri's been a prince of Persia, a man of steel, and a boy who smacks his watch and turns into ten different aliens; while Tara has repelled inter-dimensional invaders with her Lasso of Truth, fought ninjas, and saved the universe by dreaming the future. And that's just a *taste* of who we are. If you want more details, you can check out our Web sites (*www.TaraPlatt.com* and *www.YuriLowenthal.com*) or go to the back of the book to see the *Authors' Bios* for a partial list of our work.

In short, we're actors who have been working professionally for the last 15+ years, with the last six years or so heavily steeped in voice acting. Our work in voice-over has run the full spectrum, ranging from TV and radio commercials to promos to narration to animation to voice matching to looping to video games. This exciting work continues to keep us busy.

When we're not behind the mic, we're likely to be found on stage, in front of a camera, or at a convention with our fans. We love what we do and we feel that it shows.

TAKE ACTION!

We invite you – nay, implore you – to go above and beyond this book (or as a certain caped hero would say, "Up, up and away!"). To take the things you've learned here and put them into action.

To help you reach those heights, we've created a section of exercises on the *Voice-Over Voice Actor* Web site. We will add to the Web site from time to time, so check back often: *www.VoiceOverVoiceActor.com*.

We wish you much success and joy as you begin your

exploration of the world of voice acting. Good luck and enjoy your adventure!

Raise your voice!

YURI & TARA

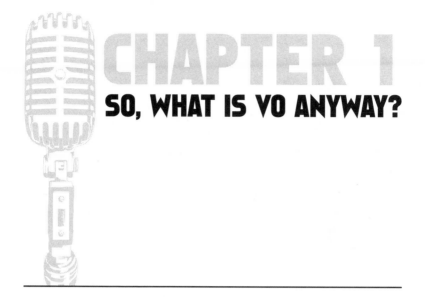

CHAPTER 1
SO, WHAT IS VO ANYWAY?

"*Imagination is more important than knowledge.*"

ALBERT EINSTEIN, GERMAN NOBEL
PRIZE-WINNING PHYSICIST

AND... WE'RE ROLLING...

In the world of voice-over (VO), *rolling* means that the engineer has begun recording, and you're clear to begin doing what you do: speak ... or in our world, yell, scream, growl, moan, bark, trill, warble, coo, guffaw, gurgle, pant, gasp – the list goes on, as you'll see. *And ... we're rolling* is sort of the VO equivalent to the film/TV world's *A-a-a-a-nd ... ACTION!*

The *rolling* part refers to when sound used to be recorded on big rolls of magnetic tape. Of course, nowadays, most everything is done digitally, and there's no real need to physically roll anything. But the saying is industry standard and it still applies. You see, here's where it begins – where we take things from a stop into motion. That's when the fun stuff really starts to happen.

So let's get things rolling, shall we?

WHAT IT IS

Well, here's what the dictionary (*Merriam-Webster's*) will tell you: "a *voice-over* is the voice of an unseen narrator speaking (as in a motion picture or television commercial); the voice of a visible character (as in a motion picture) expressing unspoken thoughts."

Wikipedia, the online (or *people's*) encyclopedia, says: "the term *voice-over* refers to a production technique where a disembodied voice is broadcast live or prerecorded in radio, television, film, theater and/or presentation; the voice-over may be spoken by someone who also appears on-screen in other segments or it may be performed by a specialist voice actor; voice-over is also commonly referred to as 'off camera' commentary."

While we love the idea of a "disembodied voice" because it appeals to our love of horror movies and ghost stories, basically voice-over boils down to this: any time you hear a recorded voice (or, for that matter, a *live* voice) and you can't see the person who's actually speaking, that's voice-over.

THE WONDERFUL WORLD OF VO

The world of VO is an incredibly creative one where I've worked with the most talented actors I've ever been around. All of them have their own unique abilities and sounds. The best ones have never left their "child-like" honesty, and are able to go into the most amazing vocal areas. I think that as long as you never grow up, have some acting ability and a healthy, passionate interest in your fantasy life, VO can be one of the most satisfying experiences you can have in this crazy business, and I have made life-long friends as a result.

PHIL MORRIS, ACTOR

WHERE CAN YOU FIND VOICE-OVER?

Disembodied voices come from everywhere. Put that way it sounds almost creepy, doesn't it? Well, not really. Think about it. Whether it's TV, film, or radio; whether it's in commercials and advertising, or cars and computers; it seems that some voice is always telling you something.

Consider all the places in your life where you hear voices. How many things talk to you every day? Your alarm clock, the radio, your voice mail, the TV, the GPS in your car, that audiobook you listen to during your commute, your computer, your Xbox, your DS?

This is good news for voice actors because, in each of those cases, we're going to bet that someone got paid to do the talking. In other words, all of these venues equal jobs that a crafty and talented voice actor could go out and get! Next time you wake up, start counting every time you hear a voice-over of some kind. It shouldn't take you long to become aware of how many opportunities there are to make a buck and have a good time doing it.

"So how do I start doing some of those jobs?" you might be asking; and we're getting to that, we promise. But before we get you into the studio to really start playing around, let's take a look at some of what's out there and where it came from. Because, as many of you are already aware, "knowing is half the battle."

HISTORY AND THE DIFFERENT
KINDS OF VOICE-OVER

Radio and TV broadcasting have used voice-over for both advertising and entertainment since the beginning of time – or since the beginning of radio and TV anyway. Starting with the advent of radio in the late 1800s and then continuing with the launch of television in 1928, voice-over has been a popular way to convey news, entertainment, and advertising. Any DJ or commentator is a voice-over artist as long as he or she is not seen. However, with the rapidly changing Internet and alternate medium programming, the distinctions between who qualifies as a voice actor versus who is considered a DJ or commentator are becoming more and more blurred. And as the thirst for new content increases dramatically each day, the need for voice-over actors grows dramatically as well.

MIC SAYS: The October 30th, 1938 radio broadcast of the Mercury Theatre's *The War of the Worlds* made international headlines – "Radio Listeners in Panic, Taking War Drama as Fact" – all without a single photo or moving image.

Radio plays, while most popular before the proliferation of television, still enjoy a wide audience in countries such as England. They are finding a new and growing audience thanks to the Internet where they are available in the form of podcasts. Not unlike listening to a book-on-tape (CD or digital download, if you prefer), these audio dramas can take the listener on vivid and detailed adventures using only sound effects, music, and dialogue. The art form remains a wonderful example of how profound and affecting a voice-over artist's skills can be.

Animation has long been the home of character voices – whether film, television, Internet, or video games. The voices created by the voice actor (VA) help bring life to animated characters who were, in turn, created by writers and designers. More often than not, these characters (e.g. Bugs Bunny, Betty Boop, Spongebob Squarepants, Naruto) are what springs to mind when people think of voice-over or voice acting. More and more animated video games and toys are using voice-over to tell a story, entertain, or otherwise engage the player as fully as possible.

Live-action with voice-over is found where recorded tracks of a character's thoughts or internal dialogue are played over the images or action, and are often used for dramatic effect (such as memories, after death, etc.). This type of voice-over is used in television, film, and theatre. For example, in the film *The Shawshank Redemption*, Morgan Freeman's character "Red" narrates, as does the (deceased) character of Mary on the television show *Desperate Housewives*. One of the great things about film, TV, and animation is the opportunity to actually communicate what the character is thinking directly to the audience. Think of how much more effective it is on the TV show *Heroes* that not only can the character of Matt Parkman hear people's thoughts, but so can we, the audience.

Commercial/Promo is a use of voice-over that's at least as old as radio broadcasting. If you can hear but not see an announcer trying to sell you something, a consumer telling you about his or her experience, people talking about a product, that's commercial or promo VO. It might be presented as a dialogue between two or more people, or it might simply be information about a product or service, addressed directly to the consumer. Think about the differences between commercials for McDonald's, Dell, or Micro Mini Machines, for example. A promo (short for *promotion*) tends to be like a commercial, but is most commonly used to promote a network or show. The announcer of the Academy Awards, or the person you might hear say, "Up next on The Travel Channel," is basically doing a commercial, or *promo*, for the network.

Narration could be considered a sub-category of the afore-mentioned live-action with VO. It is commentary that describes a scene, or tells a story, or explains whatever's happening on screen or as part of an audio program. Narration might be in the form of a nature expert commenting while you watch polar bears bound about, or it might be Shakespeare's *Twelfth Night* as read by Sir Ian McKellen. Documentaries often have someone narrating the events you're watching. If you want words and don't need visuals, you can listen to narration as an audiobook.

Instructional voice-over is similar to narration but can pop up almost anywhere. Phone systems, computer programs, and corporate educational courses are all examples of this type of voice acting. When you insert a disc in your computer and it instructs you to do something; when the elevator tells you what floor you're on; or when your GPS tells you to turn left in fifty feet; you can be sure that someone recorded those instructions. Unless, of course, they're using a computer-generated voice; but we all know those never sound quite as natural as a human-generated voice: *Wo-ould yo-ou li-i-ike to-o pla-ay a ga-ame?*

SCRATCH TRACKS
WITH TARA & YURI
OKAY, HON, I'M OFF TO MY AUDITION!
IT'S A VOICE-OVER AUDITION. WHAT'S WITH THE COSTUME?
WHAT COSTUME?

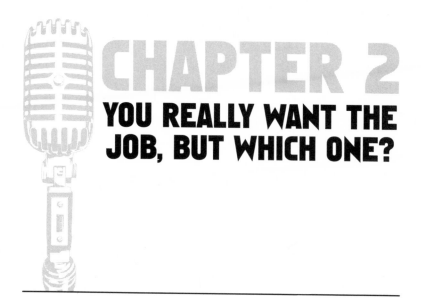

CHAPTER 2

YOU REALLY WANT THE JOB, BUT WHICH ONE?

"Variety is the very spice of life that gives it all its flavour."

WILLIAM COWPER, ENGLISH POET

SO MANY DELICIOUS FLAVORS ...

VO is a many-splendored thing. You can work in promos, commercials, animation, video games, and foreign language dubbing. The list goes on and on. Each of these areas, although similar in many ways, will have its own unique flavor. One variable is the time required for a recording session. While a commercial session may last only fifteen minutes, a video game session might last four hours, and a loop group session may take *all day*. And each one will have its own rate (and sometimes *rates*) of payment.

You may find that you're very well suited to one of these areas, or you may take to all of them. We have friends who specialize in one specific area and typically don't seek work in any of the others, and friends who will do any job that comes their way. There's no right or wrong here. Whatever works for you is whatever work you'll do.

We've given you a brief look at the most common types of VO work. Now we'll break those down a little more to see if we can give you a more detailed look at what's out there waiting for you.

ANIMATION

You may have picked up this book because you're a fan of animation. Well, you're in luck: we're big fans, too. Voice work for animation pretty much falls into two categories: *original* (where you originate and record the role from scratch) and *dubbed* (where you rerecord the dialogue into a language different from the original; in our case, English). We've done a fair amount of work in both kinds of animation. While they're both fun, they each have their joys and challenges as well as their own specific techniques.

 **MIC SAYS:** The longest-running American prime time entertainment series is a little animated show you may have heard of called *The Simpsons.*

Original

Original animation is sometimes called *pre-lay* because the voices are recorded before the animation is commenced. (*Pre* means before, and to *lay* down a sound track is to record it) More often than not, you will record original animation with other actors – at the same time, in the same room. This is generally more fun, and can actually help create better performances because you get to act and react based on living, breathing people. But it also means that you'll have to pay attention to things that you might not be worried about if you were recording in a booth by yourself.

For example, each actor will have his or her own mic, but you must be careful not to talk over someone else's line or it may become unusable. Also, while your instinct will be to turn toward the actor you are speaking to, you have to be careful to maintain a consistent position in front of your mic so that your voice is recorded evenly.

Having everyone in the same room can also help the director, writers, and producers see immediately if something works or doesn't work. Think of how many shows are successful largely because of the chemistry between the cast members. While it can be great fun and an important learning experience to work with other talented and skilled actors, just remember: you're there to do a job, so avoid the temptation of having *too* much fun. (Sometimes having a bunch of talented, funny people in a room together can actually slow things down, if you get what we're saying.) So, have fun, but make sure that the fun isn't getting in the way of the work.

Because the voice recording comes first and the animation is created second, the recorded dialogue is used as a guide for the animation. This means that when you first go in to record, you won't have anything visual to refer to while you're acting.

Sometimes when the completed animation comes back, it doesn't always exactly match the audio that was recorded. Or perhaps there have been rewrites to the script. In either case, the actors may be asked to come back for a *pick-up session* to rerecord some of their dialogue (a process called *ADR* – additional dialogue recording), or perhaps to record entirely new dialogue.

In the pick-up session, actors will have a chance to watch the animation as they record. Oftentimes, this additional session is when you'll be asked to record fight sounds or *efforts* (non-dialogue vocalizations such as grunts, groans, moans). Recording dialogue and efforts to animation that has already been created leads us right into our other category: dubbed animation.

THE DUB: A BRIDGE TO THE WORLD

Film dubbing can be described as a bridge between cultures. Its role in communicating in the twentieth century has been crucial and extends to present day. The art of dubbing has been around more than 70 years. However, most of those who have given their voices and their work to recreate the performances done by foreign artists or animated characters are basically unknown.

Cary Grant said that 80% of the work of an actor was the voice. In the twenty-first century, in addition to movies and TV series, actors' voices are heard in commercials, video games, telephone messages, and a wide range of applications in the media.

Dubbing is an international industry which is expanding due to the needs of a globalized world. In Asia and Africa, where professional dubbing has been developed only recently, new studios are proliferating, and the technology is being adopted by a new generation hungry to participate in the magic of working behind the microphone.

Times certainly have changed. Hollywood must now face competition from products filmed in places like Japan – with its popular *anime* cartoons, as well as films from Thailand, Korea, and China. Mexican, Brazilian, and Venezuelan soap operas have attained international status through dubbing.

Dubbing is also opening the doors of global markets to

French, Italian, German, Spanish, and Russian animation companies. The biblical confusion of languages finds a practical solution in the replacement of voices. Since its development, dubbing has provided the greater public a way to understand the original message from the filmmakers.

EXCERPTS FROM HIS BOOK
¿DE QUIÉN ES LA VOZ QUE ESCUCHAS?
"WHOSE VOICE ARE YOU LISTENING TO?
© BY RUBEN ARVIZU, ACTOR, DIRECTOR

Dubbed

In *dubbed animation* (in most cases coming from Japan, and often referred to by fans as *Japanimation*, or more recently, *anime*), your job becomes more difficult as you find yourself with a lot more balls to juggle. Here, you are attempting to say the dialogue in a different language than originally recorded while matching the mouth movements in the animation that has already been created; and at the same time, you are trying to maintain the *emotional level* originally recorded.

Add to all this the fact that you'll more than likely have to imagine the other actors because you'll be recording by yourself in the booth. (Because dubbing carries its own technical challenges, it has been established that recording each actor separately is the more efficient way to do it.)

Luckily, the scripts will already have been translated and adapted into English, but you'll still find yourself with plenty of things to think about. It takes practice, focus, relaxation, and timing, to say the least.

Here's generally how it works: you're in the booth (sitting or standing), and in front of you is a monitor on which the engineer will play the animation for you. Your script is on a music stand in front of you. Usually your dialogue is broken down into bite-sized pieces called *loops*. You may watch a loop a couple of times to get a feel for both the timing and what the mouth movements (or *flaps*) look like before trying to lay down the dub track.

Oftentimes the director has the engineer play the track in the original language so that you get some context from the original performance. How close you try to get to the original performance is up to the director. This process definitely takes some getting used to, and can, at times, be like juggling a ball, a bowling pin, and a chainsaw. But you will usually have your guide: the *beeps*.

Immediately preceding the moment when you need to begin speaking, you hear (in your headphones) *The Three Beeps*. These beeps are timed so that you begin speaking on the beat where the imaginary fourth beep would fall. So: *beep ... beep ... beep ...* speak! (For a more detailed explanation of The Three Beeps, you can check out "What's That Sound?" in Chapter 6, *The Booth*).

As we mentioned when discussing ADR, the skills developed in dubbing will sometimes serve you well even when you're working on original animation. And while dubbers are almost always paid less for their work, and are oftentimes looked down on by actors accustomed to working in the pre-lay animation world, the dubber's job is more often the harder one. If you can master the skills required for dubbing, you'll look really good in a pick-up or ADR session for a pre-lay animation project. The engineer will love you, and you'll save everyone time and money.

IS IT CRAZY IN HERE OR IS IT JUST ME?

My very first voice-over job ever was working on an anime dub. I landed a fairly decent part for it being my first time out, and I later found out that the producer was slightly nervous to use someone so new in the role. Luckily I had a knack for dubbing, though, and his worries quickly abated.

That same producer, however, did manage to scare the crap out of me during that first session. We got to a part in the show where I had one super-long chain of sentences that had to match up to a never-ending series of mouth flaps. Lines like that in anime can be tricky because the animation doesn't really allow for you to inhale when you start to run out of air. You just have to take one giant gulp of air at the top and hope it skids in across the finish line at the end.

Well, somehow, the stars aligned and I made it all the way through the line in one take, and managed to make the moment work, although I had no idea at first. I was still getting my sea legs.

Just as I began to reread the line to myself to see how I might improve for the 2nd take, the producer leaped forward without warning, yowling loudly like a Viking, and slapped a Post-it note on the glass separating me from the control room. *Hard.* I practically leapt through the ceiling, it startled me so badly. A second later, I looked at the Post-it, and read the letters "FB" on it. I was a much greener actor then, with zero reps in the recording studio, and I had no clue what was going on. I wasn't sure if I had messed up the show, or was being fired, or what. It certainly *seemed* bad. After I stared at the guy blankly for a few seconds, he jabbed his finger at the Post-it and yelled "*&@#ing **Brilliant, baby!**" Hence the FB.

The lesson learned being: just because you've made it to the big time, don't necessarily expect the people you find there to be 100% sane.

LIAM O'BRIEN, ACTOR, DIRECTOR

Video Games

Similar to dubbing animation, voice-over for *video games* is most often recorded one actor at a time, alone in a booth. But as with recording for pre-lay animation, there is seldom a need to record to an already created animation or picture. When you begin, you may have a character sketch or some sample *gameplay* (a demonstration of what the game will look like when the player is playing it), but there's rarely more than that to hang your hat on.

There are, of course, a few exceptions to this – the first being when you're recording a version of a game that was originally produced in another language. In that case, you may have reference tracks in the original language, cut scenes (the short movies that play in between gameplay) that you'll have to match, and strict timing concerns to be aware of.

In another scenario, near the beginning of a game's development, you may have done some work on the game while no animation was yet available; and then eight months later the producers ask you to come back and do more work on it. Only now they've got animation and gameplay to show you as a reference.

But most often you'll have very little (if any) preparation, and not a lot of time to learn about the game before you're thrown into the fire. And this is where the director will be your best friend, giving you context for your dialogue – which you will sometimes record very quickly, one line after the other, two or three *takes* per line (i.e. two or three different recordings of the same line), with not even the other characters' dialogue for reference. Other times you might get the entire script, but it's unlikely you will have the time to do much more than scan it as you jump from line to line.

A strong imagination will help you in this business. To make this stuff work, you're gonna have to imagine quite a bit. So, listening to the director, using your imagination, and making bold choices – all at high speed – are important, and together can often be the key to finding yourself on the top of the call list when a studio is auditioning and booking future jobs.

Very often these days, video games are developed in tandem with major motion pictures so that when the movie comes out, the game based on that movie is also available. Now before you get too excited about doing the VO for these video games, we have to let you know that voice actors in video games get paid a lot less than their on-screen counterparts. Why? Because the budgets for video games are nowhere near the budgets of the movies they accompany.

But now's your chance to get excited again because, in most cases, a major motion picture actor will not want to lend his or her voice to the video game; the salary paid is simply not worth the time involved. This is where you come in: the game will likely require a voice actor to *voice match* the actor from the film. See, you always knew those impressions would come in handy one day.

On the downside, video game work, because of the nature of video games themselves, can be very stressful on your voice if you're not careful. This is certainly a place where vocal control is important. If you play a lot of video games, you know that they're chock-full of shouting, screaming, yelling, getting blown up, being set on fire, and falling from great heights. And that's just in the opening cut scene.

These recording sessions can last up to four hours at a time. There have been times when we've emerged from them sweaty, hoarse, and shell-shocked – as if we've actually been through the war we were just playing at. Many voice actors refuse to do video games for this reason, and some will intentionally schedule VG sessions in the afternoon on a Friday so that they have the whole weekend to recuperate. But don't let that scare you. Just keep reading: we have ways of keeping you safe.

FILM/TV

Even though they call it tele*vision* and moving *pictures* (okay, so they don't really call it that anymore, and most of you probably watch all that stuff on the Internet anyway; so just nod and smile), *sound* plays a huge part in both of these media. And a lot of the sound work happens *after* the film/show's been shot and the on-camera actors have gone home. That's often when *we* get hired.

As we've mentioned in regard to foreign animation, you might be hired to dub an actor's dialogue into English (or possibly another language if you're multi-lingual). Some people just don't like to read subtitles, and that ends up being good for voice actors. A film or TV show might also need narration, another job for which the producers could potentially hire you – you know, if Morgan Freeman isn't available …

Another good voice acting job within the TV/film industry comes in the form of the *loop group* or *walla group* (usually a team of five to eight actors hired to record all the extra or *background* dialogue necessary in film, TV, or games). These groups join the project after a film/TV show has been shot, to *fill in* the audio *soundscape* (sounds that make up the environment). That generally means creating crowd or ambient noises that weren't recorded during filming.

Typically there is little to no scripted dialogue: the walla group actors simply make up lines based on research they've done about the location of the scene. But occasionally, a member of the loop group will be asked to match or replace a small character with scripted lines.

You see, in order to get the best quality sound on set when a movie or show is originally shot, the only people who are allowed to actually speak and make noise are the principal actors. This means that everyone you see in the background of any scene (in the coffee shop, hospital, or sports arena) is simply miming speaking and is not actually saying anything. So it is often necessary to have a loop group come in to the recording studio and fill in the voices that are missing.

Sometimes doing loop group or walla group work means adding in efforts (those non-dialogue vocal sounds) and possibly dialogue (ADR) that was somehow missed or perhaps left until later. Or it could involve replacing dialogue that didn't work out. Say, for example, that the film was shot in Romania, but the story is supposed to be set in New Jersey. Some of the actors who were hired locally may not have sounded *Jersey* enough, so the loop group may be asked to replace the dialogue with a more authentic accent.

These looping sessions can be some of the most sought-after work in the VO business. The prestige is low, but the pay is high, and the work can be profitable if you become associated with a group that works frequently.

Also, contrary to how we've described the workspace for most VO work, if you are working as part of a loop group, you'll have plenty of room to move around. The microphone is often set up fairly high in a larger-than-average room so that the actors can walk and move around and create different depths of background sound.

These different depths of sound are achieved through a

number of techniques that have their own specialized vocabulary. One example is the *passby*, where people in conversation stroll across the pick-up area of the mic to give the illusion of movement. Another technique is the similar *donut*, where the group circles like a wagon train in front of the mic, and actors converse while continuing to circle. Sometimes it's just a stationary line-up of the group in front of the mic, with every member taking a turn shouting *callouts* (shouts) that may be used to break up the walla *bed* (a continuous layer of background dialogue). The first time we worked with a loop group, it was as if we had traveled to a foreign country and had to learn a whole new language.

As a member of the loop group, you are responsible for doing your own research so that you can bring in terms and vocabulary specific to certain settings or locales that are featured in the film/show. For example, if the movie you're looping is about the crew of a submarine, you'd better ask the Internet (or your favorite uncle) a lot about submarines before you come in to work. You must be prepared to improvise dialogue realistically and within the specific context of the project. But don't worry; a good loop group director will go over what you'll need to know for a specific project enough in advance that there will be time for you to do some research.

COMMERCIAL OR PROMO

Here, we're grouping together all advertising and promotional VO. We could break down this section into individual commercial/promotional types, but let's keep it simple.

Recording VO for commercials/promo can be a fun and extremely speedy process. You may have only one line – or sometimes even one word! – to say; and then your session will consist of your going into a studio and saying that one line or word several different ways, and having the client or ad-exec saying, "Fantastic! You're brilliant! Thanks so much. Have a great day!" and then sending you on your way. Not a bad way to earn a living.

But it doesn't always work out quite like that. Sometimes, as a promo announcer for a TV series or show, you might have pages and pages of copy per session, and you could be in the booth for several hours.

And we don't want to make you think that these kinds of jobs don't require as much skill or technique as the other types of jobs we've been talking about. They most certainly do.

Usually, for this type of copy you'll be recording alone unless it's a commercial with two or more people talking to each other (often called a *partner read*). But unlike in original animation, there won't be a need for you to worry about stepping on another actor's lines. As a matter of fact, the producers will usually be looking for funny, natural mistakes that bring realism to the spot.

Sometimes the clients will be in the control room, but more often they'll be talking to you via phone patch, and only the ad-execs will be in the control room. Sometimes, the ad-execs will be on the phone, the clients a thousand miles away, and you and the engineer will be the only ones physically in the studio!

Often, timing will be a major concern because the commercial has to stick to a fifteen, thirty, forty-five, or sixty second limit, and the ad copywriters will have spent many hours crafting words to fit that time exactly. Sometimes, though, it doesn't work, and they rewrite on the fly; so always be flexible.

You may have in your head an idea of what kind of voice sells products: the *Announcer Guy* voice. Well, allow us to tell you about a little trend that's been going for the last five or more years: *Less announcery. More natural. Girl-next-door feel. Like you're telling your best friend.* Gone are the days of the advertiser commanding you to buy something. Today's methods are a little more tricky, so it'll behoove you to practice and become very aware of what sounds *put on* and what sounds *natural.*

NARRATION

When performing a narration, or an audiobook, a PSA (public service announcement), or other long-form narration, you will find that the setup is usually similar to commercial copy. Sometimes you'll be in a studio, and sometimes (especially with audiobooks) you'll be at home recording by yourself.

Most often with narration, you will either record a paragraph at a time, or just keep recording until you flub up (that's technospeak for *make a mistake*), and then stop. Still other times, the engineer will continue recording and will simply ask you to say "pick-up" after making a mistake, then say the corrected version and keep going.

Your saying *pick-up* is just an indication to whoever will be editing that you've flubbed that last bit, and you're taking it back to the last easy break in your script (usually the beginning of a sentence, or maybe even at a comma break) and starting again. You can always check with your engineer to see how he or she prefers you do pick-ups. It's just important for you to be aware that when the whole piece is cut together, it will need to flow smoothly. So be sure that you're working to maintain a consistency to your read throughout the entire piece.

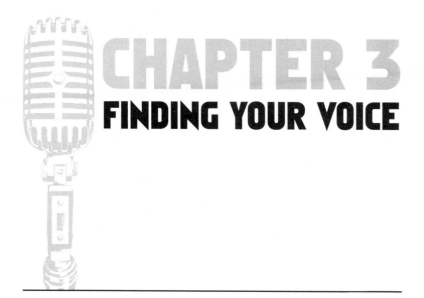

CHAPTER 3
FINDING YOUR VOICE

"When you are content to be simply yourself and don't compare or compete, everybody will respect you."

LAO-TZU, CHINESE PHILOSOPHER

It seems a little obvious, but your voice is going to be your most important tool in this kind of work. So let's talk a bit about your voice and what you might be expected to do with it.

KNOW YOUR VOICE

This is something that can't be said enough: you must know your own voice. No matter how long you've been living with your voice and how well you think you know it, you're about to start doing things with it that you've probably never done before. So take the time to get friendly with your beautiful and unique pipes. You'll learn to recognize your limits and your strengths.

Believe it or not, if you don't know your voice, sometimes

booking the job is the worst thing you could do! For example, let's say you really push your voice way out of your comfort zone in the audition, and you book the job. Well, that's great, you got the job! But now you have to *do* that voice (maybe for 52 episodes!), and if you've made a choice that your vocal apparatus can't keep up with (say, a deep gravelly voice that you can only maintain for a few minutes before you get hoarse or keel over in pain), then you'll end up embarrassed because you'll have to back out of the project, and the producers will have to find someone else.

In that case, everyone loses, and no matter how many times you apologize, everyone will remember what a snafu you caused. We're gonna bet most voice actors have a story like this; and you only need one such experience – where you risk losing your voice (and your pride) – to drive home the importance of knowing your own limits.

This isn't to say you shouldn't push yourself or that it isn't possible to expand your range. That's the fun part! But the key here is staying healthy. Start by becoming conscious of when you are speaking *on* your voice or *off* your voice. Just as our fingerprints are unique to each of us, our vocal folds vibrate to create specific vocal patterns which make up our personal and unique vocal signature. Practice creating interesting and specific characters with the voice *you* have, and not the voice you *wish* you had.

Sure, it's possible to imitate someone who has a similar sound or register, but ultimately we are each built differently, and our vocal quality is one more example of this. (You really are unique, just like your mom told you.)

You can expand your healthy voice range just as you would build muscles at the gym – by working out. Taking a singing class or voice class can often provide you with the exercises you need to broaden your range.

"So How Do I Find My *Own* Voice?"

You can start identifying your *own* voice by making a list of adjectives that you feel describe your voice and your way of speaking. Then, because we often have trouble being objective, pick five people who know you well, and five people who know you less well, and ask each of them to come up with five adjectives to describe your voice. Remind them that they're not trying to describe *you* or the way you *look*, but specifically *your voice*. If they have trouble coming up with descriptive words, maybe you could compile a long list of adjectives to make it easier on them. Here are a few adjectives you might choose (also see our suggestions in "Play to Your Strengths" in Chapter 10, *The Demo*):

abrupt	energetic	sincere
curt	fun-loving	smooth
confident	guarded	upbeat

See which of the words suggested by your friends resonate with you, especially if a certain adjective comes up more than once. That means there's usually something to that suggestion.

As you become more familiar and comfortable with your voice, you may find that you can start to identify the attributes that are specific to you. Your voice might be raspy or it might be crisp and clear. Maybe you have a slight drawl from living in the South, or a particular vocal pattern that people identify with you. Identifying your vocal characteristics is a good way to start honing in on what types of characters and qualities you might be able to bring to the table.

Some people call this description of your voice and delivery a *vocal signature* or *style*; others simply call it *your sound*. As soon as you zero in on *your sound*, you've got a strong place to start and to build outward from. It'll be your *safe place* that you can always fall back on, and probably the place from which you'll do most of your work.

Vocal signature comes up a lot in commercial VO. You might get hired because of your specific sound and attitude – which the client feels perfectly represent the product, and suddenly you're the spokesvoice for that brand.

Remember, the most important thing here is that you are discovering for yourself your own personal and particular vocal quality and sound. There are so many opportunities in the field of voice-over that there's no reason for you to feel the need to alter your own sound. Simply learn to market what you have and who you are, and that's when things will really start popping!

ADJECTIVE/ADVERB QUALITY LIST

Here's the next step in discovering your sound: create a *quality list* that is unique to you. This list is a refined version of the adjective list you've already started.

Put together for yourself a portfolio of the sounds and qualities that you feel accurately describe your natural vocal delivery. Start with the list of descriptive words that you and other people came up with to describe your voice. Add your favorite characters and even pictures of things that remind you of these qualities.

Then start listening to commercials on the radio or the VO in TV commercials. What audience is the commercial/show geared to? What voices do you connect to? Where do you see yourself fitting in? Do you think you might be better suited to play the father in an oatmeal ad or the young mom in a detergent ad? Where are you comfortable?

Think about gender, age, race/ethnicity, personality, profession, attitude, and all the elements that are central to the spot, the character, or the story. Now use all of this information to build your own quality list, one that expresses your signature style. Here are some more examples of qualities you might use:

manly	professional	bubbly	trustworthy
feminine	down-to-business	calm	sly
boyish	carefree	eager	slick
girlish	laid back	slow	honest
motherly	straightforward	warm	nurturing
fatherly	happy-go-lucky	aloof	wry

Pick one or two qualities from each column above to create a quality list. For example, are you *manly, fatherly, laid back, calm, trustworthy,* and *wry*? How can you channel *your* warmest or slickest quality?

If the suggestions above don't work for you, come up with your own. Decide which mix of words describes *your voice* when you speak. The qualities you identify make up your quality list.

Voice-over, like so many industries, has to adjust to changing fads and trends: voices come and go in popularity. When you listen to the radio or commercials or shows, what attributes are prevalent in the actors' voices? Sometimes bubbly and perky will be in, other times sexy and sultry, still other times dry and sarcastic. The better you know your own voice, the more prepared you'll be when your voice is selling.

In the meantime, don't despair. Even if your sound is not *hot,* there's still room for every kind of voice in this biz.

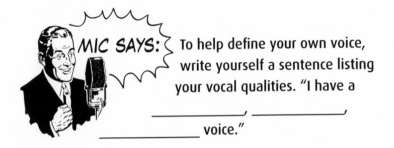

MIC SAYS: To help define your own voice, write yourself a sentence listing your vocal qualities. "I have a

_____, _____, _____ voice."

"But I Like How That Guy Sounds!"

Good! Part of developing your voice involves listening to how other people's voices sound. Become a keen observer not only of the way *you* speak, but also of the ways people around you are speaking. Being observant will help you to become more aware of vocal variations, a skill that'll come in handy when you're playing around with your own voice.

You know how people with pets have a tendency to resemble them? Well, you might start to notice that, for the most part, people's voices have a tendency to suit them. Therefore, we often find comedy when someone's voice doesn't seem to fit the character's appearance.

For example, imagine a large male bodybuilder who opens his mouth only to speak with a very high-pitched, delicate, feminine voice. You might find it funny because the voice seems the opposite of what you'd expect. On the other hand, if a distinguished-looking male doctor opened his mouth and spoke with a grave and authoritative voice, you would probably take his word for fact because his appearance and his voice seem to match perfectly.

It's the nature of our minds to make judgments and pre-suppositions about things. Knowing this, we can learn to play around with these assumptions to create interesting characters. Perhaps you have a meek sound. Would that lend itself to playing a librarian or a mousy creature? What if you have a very deep, resonant sound? Might you be a dragon or a politician? Now what if you switched it up and created a mild dragon or a meek politician?

Playing with opposites is fun. Next time you're watching a cartoon, note how many characters have voices that suit them physically, and how many "play against type." You might say that Homer Simpson has a voice that suits him; but Bender sounds about as far from what you'd think a robot sounds like as humanly (robotly?) possible, and that's one of the things that makes him interesting.

Your Strength is *You*

When I was 10 years old, I did a voice for the film *The Secret of NIMH*. I then spent twenty years acting on-camera, and my voice acting career didn't actually *begin* until I was well into my 30s and I became a recurring character on *Teen Titans*.

Working on *Titans* led to *Legion of Superheroes, Ben 10: Alien Force*, and *Batman: The Brave and the Bold*. Along the way, I've been fortunate to work with some of the greatest talents in the industry, and I've learned a great deal about the craft of voice acting simply by being in the same room with them and paying attention to how they work.

One afternoon, while listening to Phil Morris blow us all away as Imperiex, I thought, *"I'm never going to be able to do voices like that. I'm never going to make it as a voice actor if I can only sound like myself."*

Then, almost instantaneously, I had another thought. *"Wait. That's not right. When I act on-camera, I always look more or less like myself. It's the* character *who changes from job to job. Why should voice acting be any different?"*

I felt like a huge weight had been lifted from my shoulders, and I grew a level in voice acting because I was able to relax and understand what type of voice actor I was. Darkstar, Cosmic Boy, and Ted Kord all *sound* like me, but each one is a fundamentally different character because of the way I *perform* them. I'm never going to be the guy who can do interesting character voices, but I *am* the guy who can create interesting characters using only his voice.

Whether on-camera or in the booth, we actors have to know what our strengths and limitations are. We have to know what types of roles we can reasonably expect to play so we can help our agents and managers put us into a position where we can compete for them. To be successful voice actors, we need to combine both *voice* and *acting* (wasn't it nice of them to work the job description right into the title?), but that doesn't mean that we can't be a little stronger with one than the other. And when we know what our strength is, we can focus our time and energy developing it to its full potential, instead of struggling to be something we're not.

— WIL WHEATON, ACTOR

"PEOPLE TELL ME I SOUND LIKE SO-AND-SO…"

Are there already established actors who have sounds and vocal qualities that are similar to yours? Perhaps someone has even told you how much you sound like so-and-so. Great! Knowing this is a good way to start narrowing down what your own attributes are. What are the qualities you associate with that actor? Maybe you're quirky and natural like Ellen DeGeneres, or maybe you have a more raspy, sultry quality like Kathleen Turner. Either way, identifying a matching voice could help you find adjectives that illuminate the qualities you possess. And sounding like a celebrity might even help when you are marketing yourself to potential clients by giving them something they're already familiar with.

Take a look at what types of jobs that famous actor whose voice is similar to yours is booking, and point yourself in that direction. Lots of celebrities have regular clients and campaigns. Kaiser Permanente has featured Allison Janney, and George Clooney has been known to promote everything from water to phone services. Perhaps, if you're good at celebrity voice impersonations, you may even get paid to do those voices in a movie or video game.

You see (as we mentioned in the section about video games), sometimes, when celebrities aren't available or are too expensive but the client really wants them, the producer will hire someone who *sounds* like the celebrity, someone who can *voice match* that person. For example, Christopher Walken has had many impersonators (come on, you do Walken, don't you?), but one of those guys actually gets hired to sub for Walken's voice when he's not available. How cool is *that* job? So listen closely and brush up on your impressions.

A HEALTHY VOICE IS A HAPPY VOICE

You want to be able to count on your voice to be there for you when you're working, so let's begin with keeping your voice healthy. Each person's voice is different, just like each person's fingerprints. You'll ultimately have to decide for yourself what's best for keeping your voice in top form. But remember, your voice is tied to your overall health, so when you get sick, your voice is generally the first thing to go.

You probably know yourself pretty well by now and have a good idea what works for you to keep you feeling good. Here are some things that we find work for us:

sleeping   hydrating   exercising   not smoking

Of course, we're not your parents, but these things have definitely played a part in how we stay healthy. Just know that, like an athlete, you'll have to put a little time every day towards preparing your body to work.

KNOW YOUR BOUNDARIES

As we've mentioned before, when you're creating a character, be careful that you don't come up with a voice that you aren't confident you can sustain safely over the course of a session or a season. It may sound cool at first, but if it blows out your voice inside of five minutes, nobody's going to think it's cool anymore, least of all you. Remember, you are enough. You already have the *perfect* voice naturally, and anything else you are able to bring into being with your vocal cords is a bonus.

Get comfortable with your boundaries, as well as your strengths, so that when you walk through the door, you'll be at your best. Knowing your boundaries will keep you from injuring yourself, something which can cost you time, money, and potential future jobs. Remember, no one wants to hire someone who doesn't know how to take care of his or her own voice and can't make it through a session because that voice blew out on the first few lines.

It is very easy to hurt the little fibers/tissues/muscles that create your voice, and doing so can cost you a lot. Singers, actors, and many people in the business of talking or yelling a lot find themselves in danger of permanent harm to their voices. You'll want to train and strengthen your voice so that you can use it healthfully and productively for many years to come.

You don't want to develop vocal *nodes*, which are like small calluses that form on the vocal cords and can require up to six to eight weeks of complete vocal rest (not a sound!) to heal. Or worse, your nodes could turn into *nodules*, which are usually larger than nodes and often have to be removed surgically – with the danger that your voice will never quite sound the way it did before. The best things you can do are practice positive vocal health and treat your limits with respect. Always warm up your voice before a session and treat it with care.

What can you do to actually make your voice stronger? Any number of activities, from theatre and voice classes, to singing lessons, yoga, and even martial arts. These activities can teach you breath control and help you to use your voice safely and healthfully.

"I USE MY VOICE ALL THE TIME. HOW HARD COULD IT BE?"

When speaking (reading) dialogue, you will obviously be using your voice much like you do in real life. But the difference between normal everyday use of your voice and using your voice to make a career in VO will be noticeable in things like your control, your stamina, and your ability to meet any challenge the job might put in your way. Think of it like the difference between occasionally playing sports with your friends and playing professionally. You will sometimes be recording sounds and non-words (screeches, yells, screams, efforts) that might not be part of your daily routine. Making these sounds requires skill that will take practice to develop and hone.

SCRATCH TRACKS ... WITH TARA & YURI

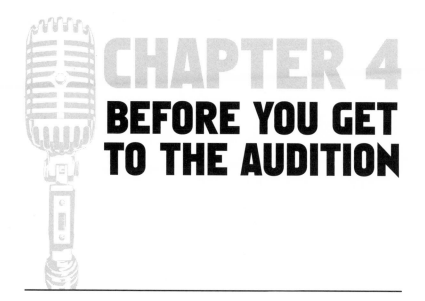

CHAPTER 4
BEFORE YOU GET TO THE AUDITION

---

*"The best job goes to the person who can get it done
without passing the buck or coming back with excuses."*

NAPOLEON HILL, U.S. AUTHOR, LECTURER

CREATING A CHARACTER – THE
ACTING PART OF VOICE ACTING

You may notice we haven't really gotten into the "So how do I go out there and book that job?" part yet. Well, that's part of our devious plan. There are several things that we think you should know before you start auditioning. One of these things is the importance of creating a strong character. We've noticed that the people who really succeed in this business are generally good *actors* first, good *voice-over* actors second. Strangely enough, when juggling all the balls of voice-over, one of the easiest to drop is the acting. Acting is where the most fun is, so who wants to drop that ball?

Creating a character is so much more than saying the words in the right order, or in a unique and interesting way. Creating a character is really about using your imagination to create the universe the character lives in, and then saying "yes, and," to that universe. This *yes, and*, theory pops up a lot in improvisational comedy (improv) and theatre classes, so you may have heard it bandied about before now.

Put simply, one of the fundamental keys to good improv (and good acting in general) is agreeing to the scenario (*yes*) and then adding something (*and*) to take it to the next level. The more you say "no, but," the harder it is to get to where you're going, and the less interesting it'll be for everyone involved. You'll find that by your being specific about the world your character lives in, the type of character that would reside in that world quickly becomes clear to you. The character's personality you end up creating this way will be real and honest, no matter how outlandish and wild the character's reality might be.

Who's to say that a talking sponge can't have friends under the sea and wear geometrically formed pants? We bet a lot of people said "no, but" to this idea once upon a time, but the success of that show goes on and on, because the right people said, "yes, and … "

Bringing a character to life through your own creativity, truth, and ability is what being an actor is all about. You get to live different lives and have experiences totally foreign to your own. Showing how much you love this part (by doing it) will become invaluable not only once you've got the job, but it's going to help you get cast. Being able to create an interesting character at an audition shows that you'll be able to create an interesting character if hired.

SURPRISE! IMPROVISE!

I do a lot of games and I love it. One director in particular just calls me in to record without telling me what I'll be doing. Usually, I'm shown a picture of the character, and sometimes, if it is an ongoing game (like *Everquest*), I'm played a sample of some other version of the same type of character (so I can see if the evil elves' British accents sound more like the Queen Mother or Sporty Spice). One day, I showed up for a session and was told I'd be playing a Valkyrie. The picture was of a nasty looking winged warrior. No problem. Then the director said, rather tentatively, "Um, the producers would really love it if she could *sing* her lines – you know – like in opera?"

"Okay," I said, "Which ones?"

"All of them."

"I can do that," I said, and watched them relax a little. I had two things on my side. First – improv – I recommend it to everyone, but this was the closest thing to an improv setup that I'd ever been handed (*You are a winged beast in battle and you must sing all of your lines – go!*). My second advantage was classical vocal training. Who knew those arias would actually come in handy some day? I was excited to see what would come out of my mouth.

And, as with any improv, I didn't have time to think about it. The engineer said, "Rolling," and I went for it. I had recently been to see a Wagnerian opera, *Tristan and Isolde*, so I had the heavy, dramatic music in my mind's ear. And for a few minutes, I felt like a voluptuous woman filling a 2,000 seat theater. I had a great time and have been back to work for that director many times since then!

DEBORAH SALE-BUTLER, ACTRESS

THE IMPORTANCE OF THE W'S: WHO, WHAT, WHERE, WHEN, WHY, AND HOW

Sure, these questions are important for reporters, but they're also important for you (assuming you're not already a reporter). They're the questions that help you make clear character choices. Luckily, in most cases you'll have a script to draw from, and it'll be chock full of answers to these six questions.

In some ways, acting is like being a detective. If you can find enough clues and put them together, things begin to make sense, and you don't have to *do* anything special. Thinking about reasons why your character says or does something (as indicated in the script) can often help you make creative choices that will help your work stand out and bring your character to life.

1. *Who* are you: what kind of a person/creature/thing are you? What is important to you? Who is the character you are you talking to, what is your relationship to him/her/it?

2. *What* are you doing, what have you done, what do you plan to do, and what's going on?

3. *Where* are you physically, where are you usually, where would you like to be, and just where are you in the telling of the story?

4. *When* is this scene/story/moment taking place and how much time do you have to do whatever it is you're doing?

5. *Why* are you doing/saying what you are doing/saying anyway? Why aren't you saying/doing something else?

6. And finally, *how* does your character choose to do what he/she/it is doing, and how is that different from how you, yourself, in real life might do it?

Often, pondering the differences between how *you* might do or say something and how the *character* does or says it will teach you something important about the character.

Between your imagination and the script, you should have more than enough information to flesh out a unique and real character. Actors often try to make choices because they feel an idea will be *interesting* or *cool* – regardless of the information they've been given. Try, instead, using your *yes, and* powers to see what makes sense in terms of the story that the writer has given you. Would that Martian speak with a German accent just because it would be kooky and fun for you to do, or because the script indicates that the only interaction Martians have had with Earth has been through German soap opera broadcasts?

And don't get caught up in thinking, "Well, I've never been to Mars. How am I supposed to know what a Martian sounds like?" Or something closer to home, like, "Well, I don't have a brother, so how am I supposed to know how that feels?"

Odds are, if you're interested in an acting career, you probably have a pretty active imagination. Use it. It's fun. Your imagination is like your voice or a fingerprint – unique. Using it will automatically make your take on a character different from anyone else's.

Even when you're dealing with sterile commercial copy, something as simple as, "Come in today for a great deal!" it can be easy to just say the words without even thinking about it (which isn't always bad). But try taking a second to get specific about what you're saying. Think of a person you know, and deliver the line as if it's just for that person. Imagine the circumstances under which you could be telling this line to someone. For example, what if you're telling your little sister who never listens; or what if it's a secret that you don't want to be overheard; or what if you're in a hurry to get the info out because the deal ends in fifteen minutes?

Suddenly, this simple, throwaway sentence has taken on a whole life of its own, just in the time it took to ask and answer the W's.

Specific choices and clear ideas on how you feel about what you're saying take your work to the next level. Sometimes things aren't clearly laid out on the page, and you can't ask the writer what he or she meant. This is where you get to make up some things, get your creative juices flowing, and harness that wild imagination of yours. This is where things really get fun.

Let's say the scene is between two brothers, and the only lines are the older brother saying, "I'm taking you to the zoo," and the younger brother saying, "Okay." The writer hasn't given you much to go on here, but nobody's keeping you from filling in the blanks on your own. Maybe the last time the younger brother went to the zoo he was attacked by monkeys, and he was left traumatized by the event. You'd better believe that's going to color how he says, "Okay."

Or maybe the older brother's never done anything nice for his little brother before, so the little brother's "Okay" is a suspicious one. In life, we're rarely indifferent about things. We almost always have an opinion or feeling towards almost everything we encounter, so why wouldn't our characters have their own opinions and feelings? Humor and drama come directly from our relationship to the things in our environment and from how we react to those things.

PLAYING WITH SPEED, PITCH AND VOLUME

There are so many different elements that contribute to how a person sounds, and if you can become aware of them, you can use them to your advantage to help you create some really fun, funky, and fancy voices for your repertoire. Start with the *speed* which is simply how quickly you're speaking: slow, medium, or fast. People often joke about Southerners (from the

U.S.) speaking in a slow, meandering drawl, while folks from the northeast (U.S. again) are more fast-paced, quick, and to the point. Play around with your speed to find fun patterns, not only of the words, but of the phrases and sentences.

Then move to the *pitch*. Generally a voice can be pitched high, mid-range, or low. Some examples of a high-pitched voice might be the aforementioned Spongebob Squarepants, or the actress Ellen Greene, or yourself after sucking on a helium balloon. A low-pitched voice calls to mind James Earl Jones, Tom Waits, Ron Perlman, or Lurch from *The Addams Family*. The rest of us fall somewhere in the middle.

One person's mid-range pitch may be your low or high depending on how you're built, and depending on what sex you are: men naturally tend to have a lower register, while women's voices are usually higher. Play around with your pitch a little and see what happens. It can lead to touching moments, funny moments, and downright scary moments sometimes.

The final basic element is *volume*: loud, conversational, and soft. Perhaps a male character speaks in a loud booming voice and is always being asked to quiet down (maybe he worked for years in an anvil factory). Or a female character's voice is shy and whispery, and no one can understand her (too many years as a librarian, perhaps). See how entire characters can develop out of how loud or soft you choose to speak?

Now look at these three elements: speed, pitch, and volume, and break each of them down into its low, medium, and high grades. The result is nine different qualities to mix and match in three dimensions. Imagine a giant 3-D tic-tac-toe board with each quality represented by its own dimension. It's kind of like a simplified vocal Rubik's Cube of choices, with speed represented by height, pitch represented by width, and volume represented by depth (see diagram below). Now pick one of the intersections of these elements (a small cube within the cube) and see what combo you get. Here are quality groupings you'd end up with if you selected each of the numbered cubes in the illustration:

Cube 1: a fast, low-pitched, soft voice
Cube 2: a slow, mid-range, loud voice
Cube 3: a medium-speed, high-pitched, conversational voice

You can come up with a variety of other combinations simply by mixing these three different qualities. This doesn't even take into account other flair you can add, such as attitude, accent, or age. The possibilities are (nearly) endless!

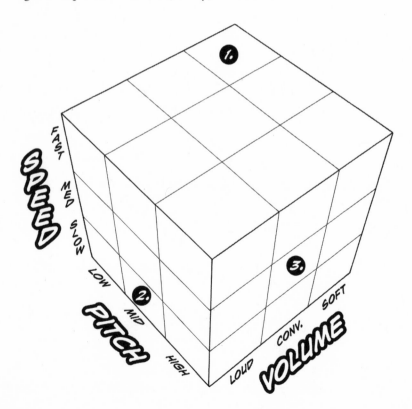

IMPRESSIONS AND TIMING

Often times, an actor (or anyone, really) will attempt an impression of someone famous, or maybe even of someone they know personally who has an easily identifiable vocal mannerism. Unless you're able to do an exact voice match, what you'll usually get will not be a perfect imitation – and sometimes not even close. But what you *do* get is a brand new character voice for your bag of tricks – one that you don't even have to credit to your intended target. You can take all the artistic credit.

The saying goes that in comedy, *timing ... is everything*. Well, it can be a pretty powerful tool when working on a character's voice as well. You need look no further than the two champions of vocal timing, Christopher Walken and William Shatner. The reason they're so often imitated is that they have oddly characteristic vocal rhythms. What are some of the things that characterize their speech? Oddly placed pauses? Stressing words that don't normally get stressed? Play with that for a little while. Do your best to imitate one of them.

Now experiment with a character that has similar rhythm patterns, but make this individual really soft spoken, with a high-pitch, and a fast delivery, for example. An interesting character, totally different from Walken or Shatner, suddenly pops up, and no one'll be the wiser as to who was your muse. *Hmmm*. Christopher Walken as muse ... William Shatner as muse. Ponder that for a while.

PROFESSIONALISM

In all the excitement of a voice-over career, professionalism can be the first trait to go. We cannot stress this fact enough: you will stand out from others by being a consummate professional.

And you don't have to know anything about voice acting to act like a professional.

Do you think the most talented actors always get the job? Not if they're difficult to work with. You'd be surprised at how often an actor will get the job just by showing up, doing the work, being a decent person to interact with, and then going on his or her merry way. Be one of these people. It doesn't take a lot of extra effort.

Be someone who is reliable, humble, polite, talented, and available. Being professional means you show up on time (or even a little early), ready to work, and ready to learn. You don't need to go to charm school for this, and it'll help get you where you wanna go a lot faster, no matter how many *E! Entertainment* specials you see about *difficult* celebrities.

Be on time

Key to the whole professionalism thing is always arriving *on time* for appointments, whether they be auditions or work. If you can, show up a little early. Once again, this simple thing will set you apart from a great many actors, and will endear you to directors, producers, clients, and casting people. They have so many other things to worry about; don't let your being late add to that.

If for some reason you *must* be late (and it happens to all of us), show the proper courtesy by calling and letting the studio know. Otherwise, not only do you send a poor signal about your work ethic by not showing up on time, but you also indicate that you don't care about their time or the time they set aside to see you.

Being on time sometimes means being early, since *on time* might actually make you late by someone else's clock. If you do get there late, don't make excuses about why you were late, how traffic sucked, how you forgot to wind your watch, or how you were attacked by ninjas. Just apologize and get down to business. Making excuses will always dig you a deeper hole, and will never get the project completed any sooner.

Be prepared

This maxim doesn't apply just to Boy Scouts, and you should put it near the top of your professionalism to-do list. *Do your work* ahead of time: read the script, warm up your voice, and make sure you've thought about whatever it is you're reading. A big pet peeve among casting people and directors is actors who show up and haven't read the script.

Sometimes it isn't possible for you to get the script ahead of time. In that case, do whatever *is* within your power to take control of the situation and get yourself mentally and physically prepared to walk into the audition, the recording session, or the meeting. Get there a little early to see if the studio has a script or sides you can look at. If something comes up at the last minute and you don't have much time at all to prepare, give yourself a quick mental checklist, a mantra, or a power pose that'll help center and focus you at the drop of a hat.

Most professional athletes have rituals or practices that allow them to focus and get psyched up. Come up with your own routine that you can do no matter how much time you have to prepare; or maybe create a short version to use when time is tight, and a longer, more involved routine for when you have more time. It can be as simple as crossing your fingers and saying, *I am super cool. I belong here*, in your head before you walk in the door. The most important thing is for your routine to be one that energizes you, focuses and grounds you, and puts you in the right headspace to walk in confident, calm, and ready to work.

Now, with all that we've said about preparation, don't obsess over trying to prepare and control every little thing. Remember, there's no way you can possibly know what's going to happen in the room; so perhaps the most important trait of all is to be relaxed, open, flexible, and ready to roll with the punches.

Be a stand-up guy

Yes, being a *stand-up guy* goes for all you ladies, too. Basically what we're saying is, don't be a jerk. Sure, we all have bad days, but when you walk into the work environment for a job, meeting, or audition, keep your doom and gloom to yourself and get down to business. Seriously. We mean it. When you're snarky and snap at your friends, you can apologize to them later. When you're on the job, you won't always have that chance.

You can go home afterwards and punch your pillow if you want. And who knows? If you're lucky, your session might help you exorcise your demons. A lot of video game recording sessions are really good for that. And sure, it's fun to gossip; but voice-over is a small town, and you never know who might be friends with whom, so you're better off not talking trash about anyone.

May we refer you to Aretha Franklin for a moment: *respect* personal space, *respect* other people's efforts and time, and just … R-E-S-P-E-C-T. And don't be a jerk. Because no one wants to work with a jerk. And sure, you might say, "Well, so-and-so is a blankety-blank-blank and they work all the time," but go ahead and trust us on this one: being a jerk will never get you anywhere. One more time, say it with us: "Don't be a jerk." Capisce?

GIVE YOURSELF AN EDGE

Breaking into the biz, much like trying to break into *any* aspect of Hollywood, is not easy, but I think there are more opportunities in voice-over than in almost any other aspect of show biz. That doesn't mean a newbie is going to walk in and land a movie trailer narration and walk out with $5000. It takes a helluva lot of commitment and dedication to the craft to start booking jobs like that – and you may never get those specific types of jobs. Though there are always exceptions to every rule, you will want to give yourself every edge you can, and so you're going to want to get training. That is where you start, and that is where you stay for a long, long time. If you're reading this and wondering, "How do I get a hold of the casting directors? I just want to tell them I love this and want a shot," and you haven't put in the work – meaning you are not a trained actor – most likely you are not going to get anywhere.

But if you do get the training, and you get mic time, and you create a good demo, *and* you are a talented actor or voice-over artist, *then* you can get out there and try to meet the casting directors and producers that can give you a shot at an audition on something. And you can try to find an agent who can help get you auditions, too.

Andrea Romano, a renowned voice director, spoke at one of our voice acting workshops at the San Diego Comic-Con to a room full of voice actor hopefuls. She reminded everyone that in order to break in, you've got to compete against the cream of the crop – the best voice talent around. (And in fact, if you can't compete against the best, then why bother?) But if you really want this badly enough to keep you on track for as long as it takes, then you *can* ultimately make it in.

The most important piece of advice for an aspiring voice actor wannabe is this: there are a whole bunch of extremely talented actors working in the biz, and the ones I see in the studio time and time again – the ones I see get all the work – are the nice ones. The ones that you *want* to work with. Those are the ones I *want* to work with. The ones who make recording sessions enjoyable and pleasant. And on the opposite side of that – those who aren't so easy to work with, the ones with attitude problems, I don't see them as much. Even if they are extremely talented. So the advice? Be one of the nice ones!

ERIC P. SHERMAN, PRESIDENT,
BANG ZOOM! ENTERTAINMENT

BE WILLING TO PLAY

When it comes right down to it, we do this – voice acting – because it's fun, because we get to play. But sometimes we can forget that. Remember to have fun, be personable, and enjoy what you do.

Fact #1: people like working with people who are having a good time doing what they do. We mentioned being flexible when we talked about being prepared. Showing that you are willing to play and experiment lets everybody know that you will be a positive force on the creative team. And that you play well with others.

Fact #2: people like working with those who don't take themselves *too* seriously. There is, of course, a line which should not be crossed; nobody likes working with someone who is *always* goofing off or being a little *too creative* with the script. But you'll get the feel for it; don't worry.

The focus of this book is the actor. However, don't let this mislead you. The actor is only one piece of the puzzle. Acting is a profession in which teamwork or group effort is definitely key. In order for an actor to perform even the most basic of jobs, a number of different people must be involved as well: writers, producers, directors, engineers, editors, technicians, designers, and developers, to name just a few (and that's not even counting the audience). So, always remember that you are a part of a fantastic and exciting team.

At the end of the day, when people have to make casting choices, there are a lot of things that come into play. Partly it is a matter of them thinking, *Can this person get the job done*, partly, *How much time/cost will we incur by having this person do the job*, and maybe most importantly, *What will it be like having to spend a lot of time working with this person?* Be a person everyone will want to spend their time with.

FIGHT SOUNDS/EFFORTS

If you watch cartoons or play video games (or, like us, do both), you're probably aware of how much time is spent on action. And for action to come off well, certain sounds are absolutely necessary. You will be making a lot of these fight sounds and efforts, which range from grunting and screaming to the dying gasp. Some studios will actually have toy weapons for you to play with as you make these sounds to help you bring as much realism as possible to your work; but most will not, and you'll have to fire up your imagination on a regular basis.

Luckily, everyone's got an imagination. And the beautiful thing is that you can practice making sounds like these at home. Imagine punching, being kicked, blocking a hit, jumping, landing, or even dying. Listen to some of your favorite animated action series or video games, and take note of the types of sounds the actors have created. See what you need to do with your voice and your body to replicate them.

YELLING/SCREAMING

Sure, we've all yelled or screamed at one point or another, whether it was at your brother, at a rock concert, or at a horror movie. Sometimes it leaves you hoarse; sometimes not. The trick is figuring out how to scream over and over again without hurting or losing your voice.

Strongly supported breathing is key when it comes to yelling and screaming. Animation and video games are filled with yells, shouts, screams, and pain sounds, so get used to making them. This is one of the reasons we really, really, really (did we mention *really?*) recommend doing vocal warm-ups and getting comfortable with your voice.

YOUR DIAPHRAGM AND BREATH CONTROL

You always want to fully support your sounds with good strong breathing, which comes from a good strong diaphragm. You'll be able to yell longer, louder, and most importantly, safer, if you become friends with your diaphragm.

Your diaphragm is a very powerful muscle that makes breathing possible. It separates your thorax (where your heart and lungs live) and your abdominal cavity. It's the thing that sometimes gets agitated and makes you have the hiccups, but it is also crucial for any and all effort sounds you'll be creating.

Imagine your diaphragm as a resilient partition of muscle and connective tissue beneath your lungs. When you inhale, it pulls down toward your toes; and then when you exhale, it rises back up, almost like a trampoline.

It's hard to actually feel your diaphragm itself, but try this: put your hand on your abdomen and take in a deep, long breath while thinking of filling your belly with air. You should be able to feel your abdomen pushing out against your hand. Now, when you breathe out slowly, keep pressing against your abdomen, and you should feel it sink back in. That out-and-in movement of your abdomen is a reflection of the diaphragm's movement down and up.

If you're having trouble feeling this movement, try the exercise again, but breathe only through your nose; or try it lying on your back on the floor. If you're not used to breathing this way (and many people aren't), this motion may feel very small or even non-existent. But fear not: practicing like this will bring more awareness to your breathing, strengthen your diaphragm, and help you develop better vocal control. And all of that helps enable you to yell and scream more safely and powerfully. Screaming well may seem like a funny skill, but better yelling can lead to a variety of voice-over job opportunities.

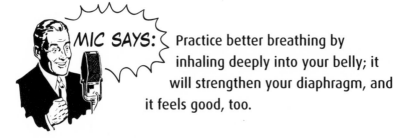

MIC SAYS: Practice better breathing by inhaling deeply into your belly; it will strengthen your diaphragm, and it feels good, too.

BREATHING: JUST DO IT

Don't get too caught up right now with *how* to breathe; just remember to do it in the first place. Suggesting that you might forget to breathe may sound ridiculous, but trust us, when you're nervous, the first thing to go is your breath.

Don't worry about your breath being picked up by the mic; just focus on breathing naturally and fully as you would when you are normally speaking. Nothing says *amateur* louder than actors trying to pretend they aren't breathing while they're recording; or worse yet, *actually* not breathing. You have to breathe to speak normally, so why would you stop breathing just to *act*?

REACTIONS

Another important part in many voice-over sessions is the *reaction*. The reaction might be a simple *noticing* sound such as *huh* or *ah* when your character sees or discovers something. Other reactions vary from gasps and breathing, to laughter and coughing, to the response you make when losing your balance. In fact, reactions include just about any sound a person might make when reacting in life. Sighs and exhales can be used just like spice to help add flavor to the spoken dialogue of a character.

Start paying attention to those little non-dialogue sounds when you're watching a show or playing a game. They're there, we promise.

NO, SERIOUSLY – JUST DO IT

That sneaker company was right about one thing: when it comes to efforts, fight sounds, and screaming or yelling, it will always sound better if you *just do it*. Imagine yourself in that situation and go all out, as if you were reacting to something in real life.

How powerful is your imagination? There's scientific evidence that your body goes through real physiological changes even when you're just thinking about something. When you *imagine* performing a physical action, your muscles fire as if you were actually performing that action.

Sound far fetched? Well, does your mouth ever start salivating when you imagine fresh baked, chocolate chip cookies all warm and gooey? Have you ever gotten home late at night, you're all alone, and you have to grab a tennis racquet and walk around throwing open the closet doors and looking under beds just to get your heart to stop pounding? That's your powerful imagination at work. And you can make it work for you in your acting.

Many athletes practice visualization, knowing that by imagining physical actions, their bodies learn to do those movements better. Tiger Woods, the golf pro, plays through new courses in his mind before he physically plays them, and it seems to work okay for him. Whether or not you believe this, the more *real* you make it for yourself, the better it'll sound and the safer it'll be for your voice.

Holding back rarely sounds as good as letting go, and sometimes can even hurt you. Really commit yourself, and people will take notice. Our only caveat is, of course, don't let *really doing it* become about flailing around the booth knocking things over. People will take notice of that too, but only so that they can avoid you in the future.

WARM-UP TIME

Since your voice isn't used to making all these fight/effort/yelling sounds on a frequent basis, it's important to warm up a bit first. Warming up your body can be a great way to get it ready for whatever you plan on asking it to do.

"What?" you say. "But I'm just using my voice. Why do I need to spend time warming up my body? It's not like I'm going to run a marathon or anything."

Well, the answer is simple: *Because we said so.*

No, wait, that's not it. Hold on; it's around here somewhere … Oh, here it is.

The answer is: *Because your voice is connected to the rest of your body, and part of warming up your voice is warming up the rest of your body.*

If you warm up only your voice, you're only halfway there. But don't worry; we like to have fun as we warm up. The exercises we suggest won't take long, and should be both painless and good for you.

First, though, before we begin any movement, listen to your body. What's it telling you today? Every day is going to be different. Some days touching your toes will be out of the question. Some days even getting out of bed is hard. But some days you'll feel like tackling a mountain before breakfast. Listen to what your body is telling you that day, that minute, that second. Work within your comfort zone, and never do anything that feels uncomfortable or painful, or anything your doctor would recommend against.

Our favorite warm-ups include working the full body, face/mouth, breath, and voice. We'll now go through a few exercises that'll help get you ready to play. We like to start in a standing position so that we get the whole body working right away, but you can adjust as you need to for any time, space, or mobility constraints you may have. After your body begins to warm up, we'll move on to your face, your breathing, and then your voice, allowing time for each area to really begin to feel ready to get to work.

Body warm-up

- Start by standing.
- Reach your *arms* up overhead and stretch as tall as you can. Lean left, lean right, lean back with your stomach out. Now lean forward and stretch gently as you try to touch your toes.

- Now bend your knees a little and roll up slowly back to a standing position.
- With your arms by your sides, shrug your *shoulders* up, back, down, to the front a few times, making little circles; then reverse direction.
- Put your hands on your *hips* and rotate your hips a few times, first one direction, then the other.
- Shake out your *arms* and *legs* to get the blood flowing (you should look silly doing this).
- Gently roll your *head* around clockwise, then counter-clockwise.

Facial warm-up

- Warm up your *face* by massaging it with your hands, rubbing gently on the nose and sinuses, jaw, forehead, and temples. (Your sinuses surround your nose, from the forehead and along the sides of the nose to just above the mouth.)
- Scrunch up your *face* as if you just ate a whole lemon; then open your mouth and eyes as wide as they'll go. Do this back and forth a few times, exhaling as you make the open face, and even adding a sound if you want.
- Press the tip of your *tongue* against the inside of your lower lip and start tracing it around the inside of your mouth, like a propeller; when you get tired, switch direction.

Breathing warm-up

"Breath work? But I breathe fine! I've been doing it all my life!"

We know, but we're going to teach you to breathe even better. The key to all voice-over work is having strong breath support, which is something that not all of us naturally provide for ourselves. Improving your support will help you speak for a longer time without having to take a breath, protect your voice when you're doing weird or loud stuff with it, and give you a better sound all around.

As we've already noted, your diaphragm plays an important part in all this. Over time, training to strengthen your diaphragm will actually increase your lung capacity. So practicing these exercises daily can help your breathing grow stronger and your breath last longer.

Remember, if you start to feel lightheaded or dizzy at any point during the following breathing exercises, take a break, and come back later. After all, we don't want you passing out and hitting your head. Even for your art.

- Breathe out all the air you currently have in your lungs. Inhale deeply while mentally counting to three, and then exhale while counting to three. Try to take in as much air as possible on the inhale, and push the air out for as long as you can on the exhale. Repeat this exercise a few times, and then try a few breaths counting to four, then five, and so on. (You should be able to see and feel your abdomen going out and in. That's your diaphragm working.)

- Breathing with vocalization
  - ‣ Try the above breathing exercise while hissing out like a snake: *sssssssss*.
  - ‣ Try again, only this time, make a buzzing sound: *zzzzzzzzz*.
  - ‣ Try panting like a dog (fast, short breaths, in and out): *uh-huh-uh-huh-uh-huh*. (This strengthens your diaphragm by forcing it to repeatedly contract and relax.)

Vocal warm-ups

Even more specialized than just warming up your breathing is honing in to focus on all the tiny muscles and parts of your body that will create the actual sounds. You will want to make sure all these tiny parts are warmed up and ready to play.

- Begin by warming up your *vocal cords/folds*. You may notice when you first wake up that your voice sounds sleepy. Humming and feeling the resonance in your chest is great for getting the voice gently moving.
  - *Hmmm*
  - *Mmmm*
- After your voice starts to feel a little less groggy, begin to focus on *enunciation*, or the art of speaking clearly. Pay attention to the different ways the mouth must move in order to create the following sounds:
  - *PTKT* pronounced *puh-tuh-kuh-tuh*
  - *BDGD* pronounced *buh-duh-guh-duh*
  - *Wewa* pronounced *wee-wah*
  - *Trills* created by rolling your tongue on the roof of your mouth while saying *TR: trrrrr* or R: *rrrrrr*
  - Rapid fire succession *ptkt-bdgd-ptkt-bdgd*
- Similar to enunciating, *articulation* relates to speaking distinctly. Let's call the moving and non-moving parts of your face and mouth that help you articulate words (lips, teeth, tongue, roof of the mouth) the *vocal creators*. Articulation is a function of how these vocal creators work together to make sounds. After practicing the enunciation exercises *ptkt, bdgd, wewa*, try to pull everything together for articulation by saying these rhymes and tongue twisters:
  - "What a todo to die today, at a minute or two 'til two, a thing distinctly hard to say, but harder still to do; for

they'll beat a tattoo at a twenty 'til two, a rat-tat-tat-tat-tat-tat-tat-tat-tat-too, and the dragon will come when he hears the drum, at a minute or two 'til two today, at a minute or two 'til two"

- ‣ "Unique New York, Unique New York"
- ‣ "Red leather, yellow leather, blue blood, black blood"
- ‣ *"Brrrrr"* made by blowing out with your lips closed to create a motorboat sound, sort of like a raspberry without sticking your tongue out (this can get a little spitty, so watch out)

- And finally, you'll want to work on your *range* (the high–to-low pitches that you can take your voice to). Here's an exercise for expanding your range:
  - ‣ *Sirens* (sort of like the sound of a fire truck): *eeeeeeee* up and down in range, starting from low to high, and then high to low

Now that your face and body and vocal creators are awake, it's time to take them to work. Oh, wait, we can't just go to work. We have to get the job first. And that takes auditioning.

We've talked a lot about getting prepared for the audition. Now let's actually get to what's involved in the audition itself. It's where your magical journey continues …

82

CHAPTER 5
THE AUDITION ITSELF

"Eighty percent of success in life is showing up."

WOODY ALLEN, ACTOR, WRITER, DIRECTOR

THIS IS THE FUN STUFF

This may sound like common sense, but if you're going to embark on this quest, you need to enjoy acting, because *there's gonna be a whole lotta actin' goin' on.* And most of the acting you do will come in the form of auditions for which you won't be getting paid – in money. Acting is unlike most other professions in that, as much as you may be working, you'll still be interviewing for new jobs almost every day (if you're lucky).

Remember, though, getting to audition is getting to act, and that's the fun stuff, right? And if you don't think so, it'll be to your advantage to start looking at it that way because you'll be doing a lot of auditioning, and even the best actors are not going to get the job every time. As a matter of fact, the best actors aren't even going to get the job *most* of the time.

Sound depressing? Hey, it can be, from time to time, especially if you *really* want the job. But don't worry: with every audition you get under your belt, you worry less. And the more you can look at auditioning as a fun part of the job as opposed to an awful, evil trial you must suffer through to get the job, the better everything will go.

Remember, every chance you get to work (whether they're paying you or not) is an opportunity to learn and perfect your craft, and of course to play. And isn't that really what we want? To play? For a living? Relish getting auditions as much as getting jobs, since an audition is an opportunity to show the person hiring (the *casting director* or *CD*) what you can do. And it may lead to many more auditions, as well as getting you more comfortable, confident, and settled into who you are behind the mic. You're building a foundation with every audition; and every good audition you have and *don't* get the job is just as important as the ones where you *do* book the job.

Casting directors are very good at remembering good actors. Good actors make their job easier. We've both been brought in for auditions (and sometimes hired) based on totally unrelated auditions we went on, sometimes years before.

EXPANDING YOUR COMFORT ZONE

We all have our happy places when it comes to acting. Some of us revel in playing the hero or heroine, while others feel perfectly at home twirling our moustaches as the villain. Either way, it's good to know where your comfort zone is and where you enjoy playing. It pays to know your strengths so you can take advantage of them and carve out a niche for yourself in the area you may be best suited to. But it's also good to be aware of your strengths so that you can take time to work on the areas you aren't as skilled in. In this way, you expand your repertoire and make yourself a more versatile, interesting, and employable actor.

It's certainly not our intent to detract from the idea of doing one specific thing very well. That's extremely important. It's just that, if that one thing goes out of style, you want to have something to fall back on. And just because you're good at one thing doesn't mean you can't learn to do other things equally well. For example, our good friend, the otherworldly talented actor Dee Bradley Baker, is known far and wide for his creature voices, monster babble, and alien squawking, and that's what people tend to hire him for. But when called upon to do so, he also turns in a very moving, believable, *human* performance.

The best actors push their personal boundaries and continue to grow throughout the life of their entire careers; filling them up with memorable, interesting, and bold characters. If you feel you're having a hard time pushing your boundaries on your own, get into a class where it will be someone else's job to give you a friendly shove in the right direction. Classes can hold you accountable for your work in a way you often can't do on your own.

Use your auditions as a place where you always push your boundaries and expand your comfort zone a little. Open yourself up to all possibilities. Widen the circle you play in.

MAKING BOLD CHOICES

Bold choices is a catch-all phrase when it comes to acting. "They make such bold choices." "You need to make bolder choices." "I loved his bold choice." So then the question is: "How do I make those kinds of choices?"

What constitutes a *bold* choice? Well, it all relates to how well you know your personal boundaries and how comfortable you are exploring them.

A common misconception among actors is that to make a bold choice is to do something crazy or intentionally weird. Freaking out in an audition situation or reciting all your lines in a high pitched whine would be a bold choice, to be sure. But would you rather be a story that casting directors tell at parties, or would you rather have them call you in again because you stood apart from the rest – as a pro? Making a bold choice relates more to being committed, specific, and imaginative in your approach to the character in the scene.

One way to make a bold choice could be to find the thing that makes the character personal to you and play that, regardless of what you feel would be the *right* way (the way that you assume they want it). Remembering that there is never really a right way to do it can be so freeing. Sometimes the clients/director don't even know exactly what they are looking for 'til they hear it. And the only way you can really set yourself apart from the rest of the actors who are also vying for the part is to be true to who *you* are; because there's only one of you. As soon as you start trying to imagine what *they* want, you'll only trip yourself up.

Another way of making a bold choice might be to take a specific quality or idea and fully explore it in such a way that you make it real, no matter how outlandish and off-the-wall the idea is. Sure, you may decide that the character is suffering from an extreme bout of the hiccups, but you'd better know exactly what caused it, how long it's been going on, how it's affecting the other characters or environment and how the character feels about it; otherwise it's just an affectation that will detract from the scene.

People love relating to things that are part of the human

condition, things they can identify with; so sometimes making a bold choice simply means finding a creative and fun way to explore the humanity of your character.

USING YOUR *REAL* VOICE

So many times we've run into people who say, "I do all these crazy voices, I should totally be doing voice-over."

Now this may be true, and there are certainly people who have made great careers out of crazy voices, leaping effortlessly from screeching aliens to friendly giants to neurotic chipmunks; but crazy voices ain't always the way to the top. People who are known for specializing in those voices are just a small part of the VO community.

Then there are the rest of us. We can do some cool, crazy things with our voices, but more often than not (in our case, about 90-95% of our work), we use the voice we speak with naturally everyday. We pitch it a little higher or lower, speed it up or slow it down, add an accent or dialect; but basically we talk as we normally do. And this is very important. Know your voice. Know how you sound when you aren't trying to do anything in particular. Know what the specific qualities of your voice are, and learn where a voice like yours fits in, as far as what kinds of roles/jobs are out there.

Don't ever fear that your voice sounds too *natural* to be interesting. Listen to the radio or TV ads. *Natural* is in: *Less announcery, more realistic, conversational, guy/girl-next-door.* Don't be afraid to just sound like you. Since each of us is unique, who's to say that you aren't exactly what they're looking for? Yuri had always hated the sound of his own voice, thinking it sounded "too much like a kid, not grown-up enough." Now he works all the time, playing kids and young heroes, and doesn't complain at all.

Relax. It's Not Just About You

The best way to learn to audition is not by auditioning. That's the second-best way. The best way is by spending some time in casting. Through the process of casting, I learned how stressful and difficult casting can be, and I can relate to and identify with the casting directors and *their* needs in a much deeper way. As a talent, that awareness gets me out of my own head and my own *need*, and *need* is casting director repellent. In addition, I learned how many, and sometimes *most*, of the determining factors in casting a role have nothing to do with the quality of my audition. I can *let go* and have fun doing what I do best; and when I *let go*, I can *book*.

ZACH HANKS, ACTOR, DIRECTOR

TAKING DIRECTION

Okay. So you got the audition. You showed up, waited in a crowded room with a bunch of other actors, and it's finally your turn. You're in the booth, the engineer signals that he or she's recording, and the director says, "Start." (Each director will, of course have their own way of saying, "Start." Only rarely will it be, "Action!" as that's more an on-camera thing. Sometimes it'll be, "We're rolling, whenever you're ready …," and sometimes it'll just be, "And … Go!")

First, make sure you've read the script you have in front of you – before you come in. Nothing makes you more nervous than feeling unprepared. And once you've read the script, hope-fully you've made some sort of choice about it. For example, if you're going to audition for a commercial, make sure you know how you feel about the product you're trying to sell, and decide who it is you're trying to sell it to. You're going to talk differ-ently to a forty year-old mother of three than you will to a six year-old boy. Be specific. Make that choice. Or come in with a few choices.

And then – this is where it might get confusing for a second, but stick with us, we're here for you – don't get too attached to the choice you've made. Having made a choice shows the director that, in addition to having some skill as an actor, you've read the material, understand it, and have an opinion. Also, a director can better direct you if you've made a choice going into the audition.

The director might like your choice, but often – and this *is* the job of a director, remember – he or she might ask you to do the scene a completely different way. This does not mean that your take on the character the first time through was not *right*. The CD may have loved your choice, and now just needs to see if you're directable.

So sometimes you'll finish your first read and the CD will say, "That was great! Now gimme something different." This can be annoying, but it happens; so it pays to have something *different* to give them. And if you don't, it pays to be good at improv. Of course, if you are having a hard time making a choice based on the material you've received, feel free to ask the CD for more information. But if you do ask, don't just ignore what the CD tells you: make sure you incorporate that new info into your work.

Listen to what directors have to say. Remember, they're not there to make a fool out of you. They want you to get the job. They want you to be good. It makes their job easier. If they've asked you to do it again, it means they already think that you *can* do it; they just want to see if you're *willing* to try it their way. And that's your job as an actor. Don't fight the director on interpretation or try to explain why your idea was better (even if it might have been).

Remember, *take the direction*. If you don't understand the

notes the director gives you, ask him or her to repeat or clarify so that you do understand. Then take a moment to look over the material with this new direction in mind. The CD should be happy to give you this time. There is nothing worse than a director giving direction and an actor not taking it. All that shows the CD is that you might be difficult to work with and unable to do what the director requests. Neither of those are things you want to be known for; nor will they help you book the job.

Specs

Even before you get in to the audition room, you might be given some direction and not even realize it. This direction comes in the form of the *spec* or *specification*, a notation somewhere on the script (usually near the very top), that describes what the client is looking for in your performance. A few examples of what the specs might include are the particular vocal qualities, the feeling of the read, and the attitude of the character.

Animation or video game auditions might provide specs that include artwork, a character sketch, a little background information, and a celebrity vocal reference to start you off, while a commercial spec might be: *Non-announcery, Ex. The "Mac" guy, Justin Long.*

Justin Long is actually a very popular celebrity vocal reference these days, and what people mean when they reference him, is not that they're looking for someone to voice match him, but that they're looking for someone cool, hip, laid-back, charming without being aggressive, with just a little bit of edge, but in no way mean. See? It's easier just to say, *Justin Long*. But sometimes they don't know how to word what it is they want. They just know they want something like ... that guy.

Whether you get a lot of info or only very little, be sure you pay attention. It's like they're giving you a helping hand … that is, provided they know what they want in the first place. We actually got a spec on a commercial spot recently that said, *Action hero read, but slightly pulled back, trailer voice but not dramatic, imagine "I'm gonna kick your ass" on every line.*

Working with the Material: Be a Detective, a Miner and a Gardener

Sometimes you get pages and pages of script; sometimes it's a single word on a piece of paper. But whatever you have, make sure you explore it to its fullest so that you can best do that thing you love: act! So now you're not only a detective, but a miner too, excavating the page for little gems of knowledge. Whether you have a line of commercial copy for a product you've never heard of, or a titular role in a new animated series, it is important to use all the tools at your disposal (the W's and the vocal Rubik's Cube, for example) to bring the material to life.

Make sure you understand what you're saying and why you're saying it. And if there's no one there to answer any questions you may have, make up your own answers to justify what's happening in the script. But above all, remember the material is your best friend and should have all the information you need to do your job (more, if it's well-written material). Even if you decide to riff on the material and throw some improv in, the script is always your starting point and should be honored.

Imagine, if you will (and we know you will, because you've got a wicked-powerful imagination), that the script is the fertile soil filled with creative seeds. Now rake it for details, water it with your imagination, and shine your energy and passion on it to grow and harvest fulfilling characters. Maybe not the best analogy, but see where our imaginations just took us?

Mining information from the page

Acting can be such a haphazard, chaotic, arbitrary endeavor, it's nice to know that there are life rafts out there for us; and one of your most important life rafts is the script. Whether your character has only one line, or all the lines; whether the page is mostly descriptions and direction, or only your lines with no context whatsoever; this is your gold mine. Now dig. Look for those W's. Does the script tell you where you are? Who you're with? What's going on? Do the other characters talk about you? How do they talk about you? Paying attention to these things and answering the W's will make your work (play) easier.

For example, if a character refers to you as a *scaredy-cat*, perhaps your character is quite timid or spooks easily. That's something for you to go on. If another actor auditioning for the same part has read only his or her lines, then you're ahead of the game when it comes to knowing your character. You can make a choice that uses the information you uncovered.

If you're dealing with commercial copy or narration, perhaps the script contains description or backstory that will give you context; and knowing the context can't help but bring out a more solid and nuanced performance. If the scene takes place *at night in a bedroom with someone sleeping beside you*, maybe you're whispering so as not to wake that person. All of these things can seem obvious when pointed out, but the trick is training yourself to find this sort of information in the script when you get it. We sometimes get nervous when we're preparing for an audition, and concentrate too hard on *what* we're supposed to say. And while that's certainly important, just as important is what's been said *about*, *to*, or *around* us.

Never overlook something in the script because you don't think it's important. Writers spend countless hours writing, reviewing, and re-reviewing a script to make it perfect. Rarely is something in there for fluff, or *just because*. Use everything the writer gives you to bring life to your character. Why did the writer choose these words specifically for this character? Try to understand the reasons behind the writer's choices. Become a psychologist and a detective all wrapped into one (a *psytective ... detectologist?* Our list of jobs that acting encompasses seems to be growing ...). Scour the page for evidence of compelling relationships and human emotion so that you can bring these characters to justice! Or rather, so you can do justice to these characters.

"So what exactly am I looking for?"

You're looking for whatever'll help you do the job. Whatever will help you understand who the character is and what the story is. Your ability to be your own Sherlock Holmes and do some basic sleuthing for the W's will allow you to make choices that flesh out the copy realistically. These choices allow your performance to shine because, even though everyone auditioning will get the same information at the start, each person will interpret that information differently.

You can tell 100 different people something as detailed as *They are in a fight with their big brother over the last piece of cake at their aunt's house on the first day of summer vacation*, and you'd better believe that's going to mean something very different to each person because everyone is different, with a different set of experiences, and quirks, and ways of thinking and seeing the world. And you'll get very different individual performances despite the fact that they each actor has been provided the exact same information going in.

Your job is to look for clues, so that you can fill in your character with the fun palate of *specifics*. And by specifics, we mean definite ideas about your character, the environment he or she or it's in, how the character is feeling when going into the scene, and how things or people might affect your character. Hopefully, reading the descriptive sentence in the paragraph above brought to life a scene for you and got your creative juices flowing. Remember, nobody else will do a scene exactly the same way as you will.

Look for *hooks* that will help you make choices. Sometimes it'll be easier and sometimes it'll be harder. You won't always get as many *who-what-where-when-why-how* details as in the example a couple of paragraphs ago. That's when you have to dig a little deeper, take what you find, and make it work for you. For example, if you are reading a piece of commercial copy, see if maybe you can find some fun wordplay or alliteration that you can take hold of to make things your own.

You'll also learn when to look at copy and just tell it like it is, without getting too flowery or trying to read too much into it. If the specs ask for a *normal, friendly,* or *non-announcery* quality, the likelihood is that the producers want a straight read, as natural and as conversational as you can make it. Let this be a clue that they're probably not looking for an outrageous choice. Sometimes a straightforward choice is the best choice you can make.

"Where do I find these clues on the page?"

The best clues are found in descriptions and in the way other characters relate to your character. But sometimes a clue is as simple as the word *quickly*.

There are lots of reasons that something might need to be said quickly. For instance, others are about to arrive and certain information has to be communicated before they get here; or you are so excited about the info that you just can't say it fast enough; or you're running late and are in a hurry to get somewhere else. What other reasons can you come up with, just for that single word, *quickly*?

There can be a multitude of motives for anything you find yourself doing in the script. To make the material come alive, you only need to decide for yourself *why* you say something, or why you say it *quickly* or any other way.

And remember, don't get hung up on looking for the *right* way. There is no right way. There's just the way you came up with. Odds are, if you come up with *your* way, even if the person auditioning you doesn't agree with your take on it, they'll redirect you and ask you to do it again. As we've noted, casting directors love it when you come in with your own ideas. It shows them that you cared enough to work on the material before you came in.

"What's on the page, you know, besides my lines?"

We've talked a little bit about reading the script and looking for specific things that'll help you do your job, but reading a script isn't always like reading a book or magazine. Sure, you'll have your lines, but to make it easier to identify where you are in the script, and to give you some direction, the scriptwriter includes mysterious notations and cryptic numbers.

Let's go about translating some of those, shall we?

In pre-lay (original) animation, the scripts generally look

like the kind of script that you would have if you were working on a play or a movie. The lines are labeled by the individual character's name so that you can tell which ones are yours. In addition, each line is numbered so that the director can easily refer to a specific line.

To help give you an idea of how to color your performance, there may or may not be descriptions in the script of what's going on in the scene. For example, if the script says, "With a thunderous roar, Roknar unleashes a salvo of rockets at Sam, obliterating the cliff she is standing on," the fact that an explosion just went off, and that you, Sam, may now be falling to your doom, might give you an idea of how you'll deliver your next line.

Sometimes, scriptwriters include very specific directions, like [muffled] or [whispering], before a line if they want the line delivered a particular way. Only rarely will they include specific *acting* notes, like [sad] or [angry], because hopefully, the writer trusts that the actor and director will come up with their own brilliant interpretation without having to have it spoon-fed to them.

ADR and dubbing scripts have their own set of notations, and while they may vary slightly from script to script, they'll generally be pretty much the same. Remember, because the performance has already been created (often in a different language), and the character has been animated, or the actor's likeness recorded to video or film, there will be very strict parameters for you to follow. You'll have to consider things like timing, rhythm, emotion, and volume, all at the same time. And because there are so many things to juggle all at once, you're sure to encounter a cryptic barrage of technical notations.

A technical notation lets you know that something very specific needs to happen in the *physical* delivery of the line, not in your character's emotional life. A good example is a pause

– needed so that the line will fit in the time allotted, not because the character is feeling hesitant/confused/pensive/whatever. Some of these script notations might look like ^ *or* MNS *or* OFF and we'll cover them in more detail in the "Mouth Movement" and "Hitches" sections of Chapter 12, *Practice Makes Permanent.*

You'll know you're working with an ADR/dub script when, before each line, there's a string of numbers that may look something like this: 00:01:17:20. This notation is called the *time code* and it allows the engineer to start recording a line exactly where it needs to fit into the show.

Sometimes there's an additional time code notation to show where the line ends (00:01:17:20 – 00:01:19:20), so you know exactly how much time you have (in this case two seconds) even before you preview the line. All of these notations are in the script to help you synchronize what you're saying to the mouth flaps that are already there. Take a look at the sample scripts we've included in the "Animation Scripts" and "Video Game Script" sections in Chapter 12.

WHAT'S NOT ON THE PAGE: IMPROVISING AT AN AUDITION

We've talked about how important the script is, how a writer has been paid good money (hopefully) to create a brilliant masterwork for you to read, and how you should pay close attention to the script for clues on how to create your character and color you performance. That said, what happens when you get a great idea that's *not* in the script? Can you just change the script? Start riffing? Add a joke here and there? What if the wording just doesn't feel natural to you? Can you change it until it does?

These are all good questions for which there is no absolute answer. But we've been in this spot many times, and here are our thoughts on it: in short, it depends on the situation and it depends on the actor.

First you have to decide how comfortable you are with making up dialogue. Some actors are very secure with improv and have no problem ad-libbing something funny on top of what's already there. There are other actors for whom ad-libbing is a downright compulsion: they can't get through a script without changing it. On the other hand, the thought of having to improv anything fills some actors with mortal terror. (There is actually a class taught here in L.A. expressly to help voice actors improve their improv skills.)

And then the question is *when* is it okay to ad-lib? In certain situations more than others, that's for sure. When you're dubbing a foreign film and an army of people has spent countless hours making sure that the lines are translated, and then adapted, and then written and painstakingly *re*written to fit the exact movements of the on-camera actors' mouths? No. Definitely not.

In a pre-lay animation recording session where the writer is sitting in the control room proudly listening to you perform his or her masterpiece? Maybe. It depends on how well you know the people involved, how long you've been working on the project, and how good you are at improv. Some people are naturally funny, but not everyone's Robin Williams. You'll want to pick your battles, because even if you *are* funny, no one will put up with an actor who improvs *too* much.

How about in a commercial audition? Definitely, yes. Why? Because ad agencies will get hundreds, if not thousands of auditions for a single commercial spot. By the time they've listened to twenty actors, their ears will start to glaze over; and sometimes it's that one audition where something is just *different*, that wakes them up or makes them laugh unexpectedly. And they'll remember that. Sometimes all it takes is a *button* on the end of your audition – an extra comment, a punch line, a laugh, or a chuckle – to get your read moved to the top of the list. In examining the commercial jobs we've booked, we have definitely noticed that throwing in an extra little *something* has increased our chances.

In the end, there's no hard and fast rule about when to improv. It's one of those times when you've got to listen to your gut.

You Never Know...

I was auditioning for an in-house partner read (radio commercial), and my character ate food that didn't taste good. He then had to make a sound as if he wasn't feeling well and had to leave. I know that for radio commercials, the word "god" is not allowed, but I managed to improvise a little and quickly say, "Oh my god!"

Upon realizing that, I figured I would do my best to completely ruin the take so it could *not* be used. I followed "Oh my god!" with "Jesus Christ!" The booth director laughed and said, "I'm sending that one." The girl I was reading with seemed worried that maybe it would be bad to send that. Reasonable. I wasn't sure either. Two weeks later I got a call saying I booked the job.

ADAM BOBROW, ACTOR, COMEDIAN

ASK QUESTIONS IN THE AUDITION ROOM

Why? Exactly!

See, when you ask a question, even if you don't come up with an answer right away, your mind starts working, and that's going to come in handy for making choices about your character. Maybe you come up with *the* answer, or maybe not. More importantly, your brain will come up with *an* answer, and that's gold.

Your performance will be richer and your character more interesting the more questions you ask and answer about the material. If you get to the audition and you're still unclear about something, don't be afraid to ask the casting director or director. It's a perfectly legitimate request and shows them that you've prepared the audition material.

Now if the director or CD gives you an answer that you hadn't considered, that's fine. But they'll probably be more impressed if you've already asked yourself the questions and come up with some kind of answer on your own. Once again, it shows you care, and that will put you ahead of most of the other actors you'll be up against who are just coming up with a funny voice and reading the lines.

The director or CD wants you to have everything you need to do good work. Remember, as scary as they may seem sometimes, *they want you to get the job*. It means they can go home early. That said, don't ask them questions just for the sake of asking questions. They're busy and have a lot of people to see.

MIC SAYS: The questions will give you your answers: Who, What, Where, When, Why, and hoW.

AUDITIONING FROM HOME VS. GETTING IN THE ROOM

Modern technology has made it possible for the actor (that's you, kid) to audition for many VO projects from the comfort of home. There are many benefits to this, not the least of which are saving on gas and saving time – and, of course, being able to record in your underwear.

However, we have found that if you have the opportunity to go in to audition live, in front of an actual casting director, you always stand a better chance of booking, for several reasons:

1. You are a warm body that the CD can meet and interact with, giving you the opportunity to allow your glowing personality to positively affect your chances of getting hired or brought back for other projects.

2. You stand a chance of getting direction and extra information from the CD, a chance which you would not have gotten by recording your audition at home in your closet.

3. You are *showing up for yourself*, or *putting yourself out there*, and making the choice to physically go where the work is, which is a nice way of energetically aligning yourself with your future goals.

Sometimes, however, auditioning from home is your only option: the client is located somewhere else entirely, you don't have time to get there, or they are accepting only submissions from home. If this is the case, just do your best to lay down a solid, professional audition that will stand out from all the others that are undoubtedly being sent in by other actors.

There are benefits (besides the underwear thing) to recording at home. For one thing, there's no pressure, and you'll have more time to work on particular moments if you want. Of course, don't let this become a detriment by getting all nitpicky about your audition and belaboring the smallest details. And while it's nice to have a CD tell you what he or she wants in an audition, when you're on your own, you're the boss, and that can be very empowering.

You'll get to direct yourself, make fun creative choices, and all the while be able to play to your own strengths. Only, be careful of falling prey to not really pushing yourself, and accepting tired or half-hearted work; or the opposite, trying to push yourself too hard. It's a fine line, and you need to develop the ability to be honest with yourself when you're alone in the booth.

Now if you aren't equipped to record auditions at home (more on that in Chapter 8, *Your Home Booth*), there's always the option of renting studio time at an outside studio. However, renting can quickly get expensive (especially if you have to do so every time you want to audition), and there's nothing like paying by the minute to make you nervous while you're working.

SCRATCH TRACKS   **WITH TARA & YURI**

CHAPTER 6
THE BOOTH

"Give me where to stand, and I will move the earth."

ARCHIMEDES, GREEK PHILOSOPHER, ASTRONOMER

Hey! You got the job! Congratulations! Now what? Well, let's get you familiarized a little bit with where you're going to be spending most of your time working as a voice actor: the studio. But more specifically: *the booth* ...

WHERE YOUR FRIEND (THE) MIC LIVES

The booth is basically an enclosed, soundproofed space with a *microphone* (mic) in it. Some booths are fancy, with contoured designs for optimum sound quality, and expensive LCD monitors for dubbing to picture. Other booths are much simpler, with just a mic and a stand to set your script on. Many have windows through which you can see into the control room, while some are nothing more than a padded closet. No matter which one you find yourself in, though, knowing a few simple things will make you feel more comfortable in an otherwise very odd place for a person to spend any amount of time. And the more comfortable you feel, the more professional you appear. As we mentioned before, that's definitely a good thing.

First off, we know the mic looks cool, and it's always tempting to touch shiny objects; but when in someone else's booth, never touch the mic without permission from the engineer or booth director/owner (odds are they'll never ask you to touch it, preferring to adjust it themselves). Mics are highly sensitive pieces of equipment and can be very expensive to replace, so the less handling the mic gets, the better. Besides, it's part of the engineer's job to make sure that the mic is positioned correctly in relation to your mouth, to get the cleanest sound possible; and they'll want to be absolutely sure they've got it set just right for each individual actor.

By the way, after the engineer has adjusted the mic for you, be sure to thank him or her. Saying *thank you* may not help your performance, but it might help your relationship with your engineer, and that's the person who's helping to make you sound brilliant.

THE PROPER DISTANCE FROM THE MIC

As we just mentioned, the mic is very sensitive, so where should you stand in relation to it? The engineer might ask you to get a little closer or stand a little farther back, but here's a good place to start: open up your hand, palm up. Now, close just your three middle fingers (the index, middle finger, and ring finger). You're left with only your pinky finger and thumb extended, much like the popular surfing *Hang ten* sign or, if you hold your hand up to your ear, the international *Call me!* sign. The distance from the tip of your pinky to the tip of your thumb is about the distance your mouth should be from the mic. You can also put two fists on top of each other to measure roughly the same distance.

An exception to this mic distance rule is when you're working with a loop group doing ADR and walla. In that case, you'll be working in a larger room, moving around a lot with a group of people, and your distance from the mic will be much farther.

Now, obviously, these rules may change depending on the type of sound you're trying to create. For example, if you're going for a whispered, or soft, sultry quality, you may wish to get a little closer in on the mic. For yelling and screaming you will probably want to back off so as not to blow out the engineer and whoever else may be in the studio.

When you speak, the sound comes out in a cone shape; so while a mic will generally pick you up no matter where you are in the booth, you'll always get your best sound if you're standing directly in front of it. And once you're in position, pay attention to where you are and how that feels. It'll be important for you to maintain a pretty consistent position throughout your session so that the recording quality matches from line to line and session to session.

How much freedom do you have to move around? The answer is ... some. You shouldn't be worried about keeping your head stock-still. You have some play: about 15-20° to the right and to the left. The same goes for up and down. There's a stand in the booth to hold your script, so feel free to tilt your face down to read from it. The mic can take it, and so can the engineer.

You definitely don't have to memorize each line and then look up to deliver it, although some people might do this, particularly if they're looking up to sync with mouth movements on a screen. The trick is to do the looking with just your eyes, and not change the relationship of your mouth to the mic in the middle of a take. Moving your head will make a difference to how the recording sounds. So, before you say the line, decide how you want to place your face in relation to the mic.

Movement only begins to cause problems in two cases:

1. when the movement itself gets noisy, either due to your clothing/shoes or your flailing about and knocking into things

2. when your movement carries you too far from the mic or too close to the mic

Either of these cases can cause you to have to do another take of the line because there are limits to what even the engineer can compensate for.

P POPS, POPPER STOPPERS, AND BLOWING A TAKE

What if we said that you have to be careful of *plosives*? Would you duck and cover? Ask for a helmet? Well, before you do, give us a second to explain ...

When you say something like *Peter Piper picked a pickled pepper*, or even the word *stop*, you are dealing with a plosive, a sound that is created by a burst of air that rushes from your mouth, primarily on *p* sounds, but also sometimes on *t, k, b,* or *d*.

Our knowledgeable friend *Webster's* tells us:

> plo·sive (plō′sĭv, -zĭv) *adj.* 1. Produced by complete closure of the oral passage and subsequent release with a burst of air (as `p' and `d' in `pit' or `dog'). *noun* 1. A consonant produced by stopping air at some point and suddenly releasing it.

So don't worry. Plosives are perfectly natural. As a matter of fact, why don't you try *plosiving* now? Hold your hand up in front of your face, a couple of inches away. Now say, "puh," or "potato." Do you feel the puff of air? Now see what you feel with "karate," or "toenail." Surely less than with the *p* words, but you may still feel a small puff of air.

Where this can *pose* a *problem* is with the delicate instrument that is the mic. Sometimes plosives can *pop* the mic, or distort the sound because of the air being blown into the sensitive mic mechanisms, or *micanisms* (okay, you caught us; we just made that word up). Sometimes, if you hit that *p* a little too hard, it'll spike the engineer's levels, you'll literally *blow* the take, and you'll be asked to rerecord.

Fear not, though. Most mics are outfitted with a clever little accessory often called a *Popper Stopper* (although this is actually a brand name used to refer to the more generic *pop filter* or *pop screen*, much like *Xerox* is sometimes used to refer to making a photocopy). It is basically a metal or fabric mesh screen that is positioned between your mouth and the mic to catch the stronger puffs of air before they reach it. These are mostly effective and help you from obsessing over plosives. But if an engineer says, "Hey, be careful of your *p*'s," or "Watch your *p pops* this time," there are things you can do to minimize the *poppage* and once again endear yourself to your engineer.

One way to fight those pops is to break up the flow of air by holding a pencil or your finger in the groove under your nose and blocking your lips, almost as if you were going to *shh!* someone. Try some plosives again, with and without your finger/pencil in place. Do you feel the difference?

Another way to lessen a *p pop* is to try to slightly swallow the sound, thereby eliminating some of the air you release; but make sure that in doing this, you don't cause the word to become unintelligible.

A third method for taming plosives involves a little something called going *off-axis*. To do this, you'll just need to point your mouth a little to the left or a little to the right of the mic so that the air isn't going straight into it. Be careful, though: you don't want to turn *so* far off-axis that the mic doesn't pick you up well enough.

MIC SAYS: A finger or a pencil can help stop a pop.

WATCHING YOUR VOLUME

Some of the techniques for minimizing plosives can also be used to keep from blowing out the engineer's levels when you're going to be suddenly, and without warning, LOUD. If you're going along at a very conversational volume, and then all of the sudden you scream or shout, odds are you're going to take the engineer by surprise and he or she won't be able to bring the sound levels down in time. So, if suddenly you realize that you're going to be loud and the engineer might not see it coming, throw that loud stuff a little off-axis, by turning slightly off-mic (for you dancers out there, a little *Twist and Shout*), or by backing off the mic a step or two to compensate for the sudden boost in volume.

This is a lot to be thinking about right now, so don't become obsessed with this stuff when you get in the booth. We're telling you most of these things to help increase your general awareness, comfort, and confidence; not to have you create a list and memorize it.

The bottom line is that you'll pick up these behaviors and techniques as you work, and the engineer will be there to tell you if you need to adjust anything as you go. The info we've given you is all just stuff for you to keep in the back of your mind, so that when it does come up, you won't be completely caught off guard.

MOUTH NOISES: CLICKING, SMACKING, AND GURGLING

We keep telling you that the microphone is a very sensitive instrument. What we haven't mentioned before – but what you may very well be aware of – is that your body makes noises, sometimes even when you don't want it to, and your good buddy *Mic* hears every one. Many of these noises you've learned to hide from the public at large, and some noises you may not even hear yourself. But you can be sure of one thing: the mic will pick them up. Picking up sound is what the mic was designed for. Let's talk about some of the more popular sounds that occasionally creep into a recording.

Clicking (a mouth click) is the bane of a VA's existence. Mouth clicks happen when your mouth becomes too dry and the mic begins to pick up the sounds of your lips, cheeks, and tongue. Sometimes this is called *being smacky*. A swig of water can help with this sometimes, but saliva is your best lubricant, and water can actually dry out your mouth even more if you already have dry mouth; or, just as bad, make you *splashy* or too *wet* sounding.

But fear not! There is a magical cure. To help an actor with a severe case of *clickiness*, most studios will have on hand this cure: The Mighty Green Apple. And by green, we mean Granny Smith, not Golden Delicious; let's just be clear about that. One bite, and the clicks disappear as if they never existed. Why does this work? Why only Granny Smith apples? It's a mystery. (And by that we, of course, mean magic. Yuri thinks it has something to do with little apple elves who erase the sounds as you make them; but then again, that's our Yuri.)

Actually it's the chemical composition of the Granny Smith's juice that does the trick, so you don't even have to *eat* the apple to get the benefits. Simply biting and sucking will suffice. And once again your engineer will thank you, because if there's anything worse than clickiness, it's having to listen to a super-amplified actor chewing and swallowing and trying to clear his or her mouth of apple bits.

Tara once had a session in which, between *every single line*, it was necessary for her to take a bite of apple since she was recording a quiet, whispery character. She was in really close to the mic, and *everything* was being picked up. So it was a trade-off: no more clicks, but the engineer had to listen to her munching apples all day – in addition to hearing the burbling, gurgling sounds that her stomach made as it fought to digest the onslaught of Granny Smith!

One way to minimize this kind of trouble is to make sure that you're staying really well hydrated at all times. Basically, drink water as often as possible. This will keep your vocal folds/cords ready to work, and your mouth well-lubricated and ready to talk. And don't wait until you show up to work. It takes time for water to truly circulate throughout your body after you've ingested it. Drink water starting the night before so that your voice and body are ready to stand (or sit) in a dry booth and talk (or scream) for several hours at a time.

We actually have a (not particularly clever) mnemonic that helps us: ADW – Always Drink Water (we know, we *told* you it wasn't particularly clever). This means that if anyone at all offers you water, you have to say "yes" *and* drink it (unless you suspect that they might be trying to poison you). Drinking more water every day may have serious side effects, though: improved health, vitality, and a serious need to go pee more often, have been known to result from hydrating. But don't confuse *hydrating*, with *drinking liquids*. The latter may not necessarily mean the former.

Beverages such as alcohol and coffee (or any caffeinated beverage, really) actually dry you out. You might want to avoid drinking them right before a session, or even the night before a session. Warm herbal teas (without caffeine), on the other hand, can have the opposite (and positive) effect of soothing and warming up the voice. Add a spoonful of honey and you're good to go.

And while we're on the topic of foods, try to avoid dairy products right before a session. They make you phlegmy, which, in addition to just sounding gross, can also choke you up a bit and make for bad recording.

MIC SAYS: Green apples keep the clicks down.

NOT JUST YOUR MOUTH: SHUFFLING, RUSTLING, AND SQUEAKING

Let's assume for a moment that the noises from your mouth are coming out exactly the way they're supposed to: you're not out of the woods just yet. Hey, if all you had to do was move your mouth, you'd be fine. But, what with all the acting you're doing at the same time, it's hard to keep the rest of your body still; trust us. And moving body parts = more noise.

Like what, you ask? Well, let's start from the top and move our way down: first, ditch the baseball cap. If you *must* wear it, turn it around so that the brim's in back. A baseball cap will actually change the sound quality of your recorded voice because of how the sound waves bounce off the brim. Satiny shirts, or jackets made of crinkly or otherwise noisy material? Definitely a no-no. Same goes for pants, and that includes corduroys. And anything jingly that you have hanging off your clothes. And finally, your shoes: squeaky soles or squeaky leather will get picked up every time.

Sure, you look great in all your stylish finery, and standing there in front of the mirror you don't hear a thing. But in the booth, you move whether you like it or not. Hey, we've all gotta breathe. And as we've said already many times before, the mic is built to pick up the slightest sounds. Do you really want to be self-conscious about breathing and rustling and squeaking when you should be concentrating on having fun?

Tara once learned the hard way that fashion and VO don't always mix when she went into a session with a beautiful new skirt. It was bright and had an overskirt with little mirrors all over it. Little did she realize how noisy hundreds of little pieces of glass clinking together could be – until the sound was amplified in her headphones, of course. She sounded like one of those bead curtains from the 1960s. It got so bad that she had to roll up the top layer of the skirt and tie it behind her so that the rustling and jangling wouldn't be picked up on the recording. Boy, did she feel like an amateur. She never let *that* happen again.

Once, in another session, Yuri had to lend another actor his hoodie because she had to remove her noisy shirt and had nothing else to change into. At least, that's his story ...

So before you leave the house, dance around a little first. If *you're* hearing something, the mic's *definitely* going to hear it. Ditch the noisy article(s) of clothing and move on. You can be fashionable later. Your ideal voice-over wardrobe is going to be comfortable, soft things like tee shirts, jeans, and sneakers. It's always good to have a sweatshirt or something long-sleeved with you as well. Sometimes even when it's hot *outside*, the booth can be like an icebox. You want to be prepared, and you definitely don't want to catch a cold.

And not just your clothes, either ...

Now that you've gotten a handle on your noisy wardrobe, we're going to give you one last thing to keep quiet: your script. Unless the studio has set it up so that your script is displayed on a screen in the booth, your script will likely be in the form of pages on a stand in front of you. And you're likely going to have to turn those pages at some point. And the mic will hear that. So as you're standing in the booth, take a moment to see if you can arrange your pages in a way that allows you to read as many as possible without having to fiddle with them, thereby eliminating noise. If you must turn pages while you're recording, that's perfectly all right; just make sure that no one is talking as you do it – not you or anyone else. As quiet as you think you're being, odds are that mic is going to hear the page turning, and the engineer's going to ask for another take.

FULL OF HOT AIR

While working on a show for Hasbro I was asked to schedule a female VO actress to do a simple pick-up. In order to spare her blushes, let's call her "Jane." It happened that Jane was working near the studio, and had just finished her post-lunch session. As she only had one loop to pick up, she offered to come over immediately.

Now ... it just so happens that the male VA who was working in the booth, let's call him "John," had eaten a spicy lunch, thinking he would have *single occupancy* of the booth for the whole afternoon.

When Jane arrived, John seemed very shy about letting Jane into the booth, and if memory serves me correctly, he was a little more animated than usual – you know: waving his arms around a lot.

When we finally enticed John out of the booth, Jane ran in

... only to run out again a moment later shouting, "Oh my god. It smells like something has @*%!ing died in there."

It took ten minutes, a lot of wafting, and a personal appearance in the booth to convince Jane that it was safe to go back in the booth.

And so you see the old phrase is right: comedy is all in the timing!

— MARK A. TODD, WRITER, DIRECTOR

"WHAT'S THAT STUFF IN THE BOOTH WITH ME?"

Every booth in every studio is going to be a little different. Some might be bigger and some might very well be the size of a small coat closet. Some booths may be stacked to the gills with equipment, and some you may share with only the mic. So rather than list specifics, why don't we just paint a general picture of what a typical sound studio or recording booth might have in it. And, as always, technology advances at a lightning pace; so who knows what'll be in the booth when you finally step in to work.

The stand, the cans, the mic and you

Hey, look! It's some of your old friends: mic, mic stand, and pop screen! The old gang is back together again. These guys'll almost always be there, in one form or another, no matter what studio you're recording in. Remember, though, as familiar as you've become with these guys, don't get *too* familiar and go moving them around. That's still the engineer's job. Besides: it gives the engineer an excuse to come in and chat with the actor for a minute while adjusting the position of the mic for you.

Now, the mic stand isn't the only stand you'll encounter on your journey. Your *script stand* (usually just called *the stand*) looks like a music stand (and more often than not, is one). The script stand is where you'll rest your script while you read from it. (We may not have mentioned it thus far, but one of the perks of voice acting over on-camera or stage acting, is that you will rarely, if ever, have to memorize your lines. You'll always have your script open in front of you.)

Some studios these days have all but done away with a printed script, opting instead to present your script on a monitor or screen which is visible from where you're standing in the booth. But if there is a script stand, generally it is something you can touch without making your engineer nervous. But remember, depending on how high or low you set the stand, you can actually change how the mic picks up your voice. So if you're going to adjust the height of the script stand, do it before the engineer comes in, or while he or she is in the booth setting up for you.

That reminds us, when they're adjusting the mic to the right height for you, be sure you're taking pretty much the same stance as the one you'll take while you're recording. Yuri has a tendency to settle into an *action pose* over the course of a session, and if he doesn't stand that way when the engineer's setting the mic at the beginning, the engineer inevitably has to come in to correct the mic position later on in the session.

This seems to be a good place to mention standing versus sitting. When you're recording, you can usually choose between sitting and standing. It's a matter of personal preference. Some people always sit and some always stand. We each sit sometimes and stand sometimes. Tara finds that standing helps her keep her energy up, which for certain shows or games can be extremely important, especially if there's a lot of action. On the other hand, if she knows she's going to be in a narration session for four hours, she'll do the session seated.

We talked about movement in the booth at the beginning of this chapter. The same rules apply whether you're sitting or standing. Keep your face in that sweet spot and the engineer will appreciate it. If you don't, then both of you will be doing extra work.

Oh, wait! Here's a new friend. Allow us to introduce to you a booth companion that may be familiar to you from your outside life: the *headphones*. Odds are, unless you're a DJ, *these* headphones (sometimes called *cans*) will be a little more heavy-duty than the ones you hook up to your MP3 player. But they work pretty much the same.

These headphones will allow you to hear both the engineer and director when they're speaking to you from the control room, as well as hear the sound of your own voice when you're recording. Usually they're plugged into a headphone amplifier, a little box with a volume dial on it. You are, in fact, allowed to touch *this* dial, so feel free to adjust the volume to a level that is comfortable for you.

Some voice actors like to keep the headphones over both ears, while some like to leave one side off. Once again, this is a personal preference. Experiment with them both ways, and see which feels better to you. In some sessions you might not use headphones at all, the director preferring to use *talkback*. Talk-back simply means that there's a speaker in the booth, through which the director and/or engineer will communicate with you. (Sometimes the term talkback is also used to mean communicating from the control room through *either* the headphones or a speaker system.)

Try practicing with the headphones all the way on, all the way off, and one-on/one-off. Your voice will sound different to you depending on the configuration of the headphones, and you want to choose the one that's most comfortable for you whenever possible. We know some actors who prefer wearing both headphones so much that, even when there are no headphones in the booth, they cup their hands around their ears to simulate the way they hear their own voices when the headphones are on.

Don't worry if you get into the booth and there aren't any cans. Some booths are set up to have talkback engaged through in-room speakers, so there is no need to use headphones at all. Don't get too accustomed to using them or not using them, so you can be flexible no matter what type of studio you're working in.

"What's That Sound?"

Don't worry. You're not hearing things that aren't there. That beeping sound in your headphones? That's a more specific way of saying, *We're rolling*. It's an audio cue for you to begin speaking. As we mentioned in the section on dubbing, more often than not, the cue you hear will be The Three Beeps: *beep ... beep ... beep ...* after which you will begin, as if on the imaginary fourth beep. This can be very important for timing, particularly in the case of foreign language or ADR dubbing. The director wants your dialogue to sync up with the already existing mouth movements, so the engineer sets up the beeps to help you start on time.

The Three Beeps are equally spaced apart. The reason there are *three* is that three's the perfect number to give you an opportunity to get accustomed to the timing. So, you'll hear: *beep ... beep ... beep ...* and when the *fourth* beep would come in, you start speaking. Once again, this is most important when there is a timing issue, such as in dubbing. Otherwise, you may just hear the director saying, "Okay, we're rolling. Whenever you're ready, go ahead."

So you're standing or you're sitting; you've got a script on a stand in front of you or you're reading it off a monitor; you may be trying to time something to a video image; you've got your headphones on (or half-on/half-off); you're waiting for beeps; and you're in your stance. That's a lot of stuff to be thinking about all at once, and increasingly tricky as soon as you remember that you also have to be *acting* at the same time. (It may sound a little like patting your head and rubbing your belly at the same time, while also spinning in a circle, eating an ice cream cone, and composing a symphony; but it gets easier.) After a little practice, the balancing routine will become a part of your magic act and you'll find yourself able to focus on your performance while the rest of the stuff just takes care of itself.

BE A CONSCIENTIOUS CAMPER

One last note on the booth. Treat it like a campsite: always leave it in a better state than you found it. Clean up after yourself, and if the actor before you left a half empty water bottle or other trash behind, toss it on your way out. It may seem like a little thing, but it shows respect for your space, what you do, and the people you work with.

People often joke about how voice actors can go to work in their pajamas if they want because it doesn't matter what they look like. While we've never actually seen anyone show up in their PJs, we've both seen many an actor show up to work in comfy sweats and a well-loved tee shirt. Make sure they're not *too* well loved, though. Remember, another actor's going to be in that booth after you leave. You don't want to become associated with the smell you leave behind. That goes for strong perfume or cologne, too. The person who records after you might be allergic or just plain sensitive. So this might be the only time you *don't* want to come in smelling like a rose. Or anything else for that matter.

But the booth is a small place, and only part of where you'll be working. So what goes on beyond that door? Let's take a look ...

CHAPTER 7
THE STUDIO

"The way a team plays as a whole determines its success. You may have the greatest bunch of individual stars in the world, but if they don't play together, the club won't be worth a dime."

BABE RUTH, U.S BASEBALL PLAYER

"HOW'S THE STUDIO DIFFERENT FROM THE BOOTH?"

For our purposes, let's define a *studio* as anywhere you go to record. The booth is part of the studio. But, wait, there's more. In the studio, for every booth, there's a control room, where the director, engineer, and possibly others (engineer's assistant, director's assistant, clients …) are working hard at the same time as you. Remember, like most creative endeavors in the entertainment industry, the actor's job is just one part of the whole.

We've worked in all kinds of studios, but the basic setup as far as you, the actor, are concerned, is the same. There will always be some type of control room and some type of booth. Some studios will consist of nothing but those two areas, while others might have a fully stocked kitchen and catering department. Some studios might be housed in a massive compound with multiple rooms, while some might only be the garage at someone's house. But don't let size fool you. As long as you've got a good director, engineer, and equipment, you're ready to rock ... and *roll*.

Don't Psych Yourself Out

There will be times when you're in the booth recording, and you've just laid something down (i.e. just recorded something), and the folks in the control room are working. If you're in a studio that has a window between the booth and the control room, you can see those folks; but often talkback is turned off while they work (usually to spare you having to listen to them). This is totally normal, and you'll have to learn not to obsess over what they're talking about in the control room. Due to the tenuous and often stressful nature of our business, actors can have a tendency to suspect the worst in a given situation.

So think about it: you're working, you're working, the director's making jokes, you're all laughing, everybody's happy, then abruptly the line goes dead and you're cut off. You can see that it's suddenly serious in the control room. The engineer's talking to the director, the director's talking to the client, the client's talking to their boss in Brussels over the phone, and you can't hear a word of it. All you hear is your breathing and every other little sound in the booth, amplified in your headphones. It's enough to rattle anyone.

They've got to be talking about you, right? *Right?* Well, the truth is, probably not. Remember, there's more to this process than just you, and odds are they've cut you out of the discussion so they won't bore you with technical stuff.

Also, turning off the talkback is the director's way of protecting you from all that outside stuff that might get in the way of your acting process. A good director knows when to let you listen to what's going on in the control room and when not to. Directors check in with the client occasionally to see if things are going in the right direction, and they should leave you out of that discussion. Most of the time, producers and clients don't have a clue how to communicate with actors. The director knows this, and would much rather interpret the information from the client, and communicate it to you in the best way possible. Sometimes the director is working with the engineer because everyone really liked your performance, but they need to do some technical tweaking to make it perfect.

In other words, if you can't hear what's going on, take a deep breath, relax, and assume the best. No news is good news. If the director and/or client want something different from you, they'll just ask.

Some sessions are directed via *phone patch* because the director or the client is off site somewhere, meaning not in the same building or even the same country! Ah, the wonders of modern technology ... In a phone-patch session you'll have to be even more comfortable with silence and waiting, as the client in Montreal may be talking to the engineer in the control room who may be talking to the director in New York who may be talking to the actor working opposite you who's actually in another studio downtown because they couldn't make it over to where you're recording. So enjoy the silence. It's golden.

It's All in Your Head

So here's a story I've told so many times that we decided it deserved a place in this book. I was in the studio to record a tag for a TV commercial. It was literally six words. I thought I'd be in and out in fifteen minutes tops, even if they had me do it several different ways to make sure they had their bases covered. Almost half an hour into the session, I'm sweating. They've had me do it what seemed like a thousand different ways, so obviously they're still not getting what they want. I'm alone in the booth and they've cut the talkback, but I can still see them through the glass.

I try to focus on the script, the floor, anything to keep myself from obsessing over what they might be talking about, but it's no use. I see the director talking heatedly to the client. They go back and forth. The engineer turns around to give his two cents. I don't know what they're saying, but it's not good. *I can tell.* "I'm about to get fired," I think. An assistant reaches for a phone.

I figure at that point they're getting on the phone to do one of two things: 1) Call my agent to complain about how bad an actor I am, or 2) Get another actor in to replace me. Maybe both. What was I going to do? My life was over. Word would get out that I couldn't hack even six words of commercial copy and I'd be back to temping, working in an office where I'd — the talkback clicked on. They must have seen my pitiful face looking out from behind the glass.

The director says, "Hey, sorry for the wait, Yuri. We totally got it, you're brilliant, thanks. We were just arguing over what we were going to get for lunch today. You want us to order you something?" I learned two things that day: 1) Never assume you know what they're talking about on the other side of the glass, and 2) If you are going to assume, assume it has something to do with Thai vs. Mexican.

— Yuri Lowenthal, Actor

"WHAT DO THOSE GUYS/GALS DO ANYWAY?"

Just what do those people across the glass from you do? Any number of things, but generally they fall under the headings *director, engineer, producer,* or *client.* Each one is responsible for a different part of the process, and together, with your help, they assemble like the Voltron lions to form a mighty project.

So which is which? Not always easy to tell at first glance, and you might not always have everyone on this list in the studio with you, but odds are, whoever talks to you *most* will be the director. The engineer will also be pretty easy to pick out. That's the person who comes in and makes sure that your mic is set correctly, and is also working the control panel and instruments. All those other faces are up for grabs: producer, client, ad-executive, writer, game designer, or maybe even the client's nephew. And you may or may not be introduced to these people.

If all goes smoothly, the director and engineer might be the only two people you talk to while you're in the booth. Communication with anyone else should go through the director, although occasionally, for a moment, the director will turn over the talking to a producer or designer who knows the show/game/product best.

We know that this is a lot of different people to remember, but the most important thing to keep in mind is: none of these people are against you, and everyone is rooting for you. Sure, you'll occasionally encounter someone having a bad day; but just remember to take it in stride, and never let your work be affected by someone else's having gotten up on the wrong side of the bed that morning.

THE DIRECTOR

It's the voice director's job to know the script and the story (or product) and work with the actor (or cast) to create a performance that best serves the project. He or she will give direction or adjustments directly to the actors to keep them on track, and may experiment in different directions to capture the best performance possible. A skilled director will be able to communicate his or her vision to an actor without resorting to a *line-read* (e.g. "Repeat after me." ... "Say it like this."), and will work *with* the actor to create the performance. But if you get a line-read or a frustrated director, just take a breath, relax, and work through it.

You also must remember that, besides dealing with you, the director has to answer to the producer or client (who may even be there in the same room); as well as work with the engineer to make sure that your performance is recorded and useable. Since the director is your connection to the rest of the team, forging a solid and trusting relationship with him or her should always be a priority when starting a project.

This doesn't mean working hard to become the director's bestest friend ever. Rather, the best way to foster a good relationship is to listen, ask questions when you need to, and be responsive to the direction you are given. Keep in mind that a director who likes working with you on one project will likely bring you in on future jobs because they are familiar with your work, know you're easy to work with, and know you can get the job done.

If you have worked with the director before, and feel comfortable occasionally asking for an extra take or to try something different, go for it. But once again, remember to pick your battles. An actor who wants take after take to get it *perfect* even though the director was happy with the first take, slows everything down, and will stop getting hired after a while.

From the Director's Chair

I'm probably considered a cranky director. I want actors to take their jobs as seriously as I take mine. Whether interactive games or series animation, a lot has to be accomplished in a short amount of time. So I'm not a big fan of playtime ad nauseam. If the actor comes in for a gig, I want them to already be acquainted with the material in advance so we can just "go"... no table read. Questions or story problems are worked out at the top of the session, and we basically "rehearse on tape," taking whatever is working for the print, and doing pick-ups or adjustments after we complete a run. So the more people are prepared, the faster we can get to making our magic! I ask *a lot* from actors. I rarely settle, and I thrive on getting every option out of a read.

In a recording session, direction may change and often does. So being flexible is a must. And *listening*. The other side of the glass is often a mixture of writers or producers working out their business. Actors should never think it's "them"! And, the person directing may not always be a great communicator or "an actor's director." It doesn't hurt for the actor to be a patient mind reader, or even a clever "second guesser"! When the timing is right, *input* from the actor can also be helpful ... Someone might have an idea for their character or a line rewrite that can make a scene better.

I often talk in *CliffsNotes*. Once the actor has, hopefully, done their homework, I can just give them the essentials before a scene or line ... not talk it to death, losing all freshness in their delivery (or mine). Just remaining open to everyone and everything creatively in a session is crucial. I'll never stop appreciating the wonderful talent that has come my way for decades now. The ones I revere are *not* celebrities. Yet. They should be.

— Ginny McSwain,
Casting Director, Director

Direction from near, direction from afar

When you are in the recording session, there are two ways that your director will communicate with you. The first and most common way in animation or video game work is for the director to be physically in the control room. He or she will most likely be sitting next to, or at least near, the engineer (and sometimes producer); and will use a *talkback button* to communicate with you through the glass. This is just a button that, when pushed by the director, allows you to hear what's happening in the control room (through headphones or a speaker – as we've already discussed). Having the director physically there is great because, even when the talkback button is off, the director can still *see* you through the glass; and *face time* with directors – if they like your work – can get you hired again.

On the other hand, sometimes (most often in commercial or promo recording sessions) you will find yourself in the booth, and the only other person on the other side of the glass is the engineer ... while the producer, director, and client are on a phone line talking to you (we've mentioned this before). The callers are then patched through to your headphones so they can hear you and direct you – even though some or all of them may be physically halfway across the world. A lot of the time, the ad-execs are located in Chicago or elsewhere, and the work is recorded in NYC or L.A. The phone patch makes it possible to get everyone together *in the room* in spite of great distances.

For all intents and purposes, a phone patch will *feel* the same to you in the booth as when you're using talkback with the director in the room, as all the info will be coming through your headphones or speakers. But with a phone patch, you won't get face time with the director/client. You could go a year working with the same people, and never even know what they look like.

Translating some directing terminology

You will, in your VO journey, encounter some unfamiliar terms. Some of them may sound familiar but then end up having totally different meanings than you're used to. Here are examples of a few of the more common expressions:

- "Gimme a *slate*," or "Slate your name."

   This basically means that the producer and director want you to say your name (usually right before you begin an audition) so that they can record it; then they'll have it with your audition so they can keep track of whose audition it is. You will often follow your name with the name of the character you're reading for. You can keep it as dry as saying:

   Yuri Lowenthal, Cowboy Number Three.

   Or you can give it some character:

   Hi, this is Yuri Lowenthal, and I'm reading for the part of Cowboy Number Three, yeee-haahh!

   During a recording session, the engineer usually records a different kind of *slate* between each take so that he or she can keep track of the takes for later. To lead into this slate, the engineer says something like this: "We're rolling on Take Forty-Two," or "This is Take Seventy-Four." That's usually your cue to start speaking your line.

- "Can I get an *ABC take*?"

   Directors sometimes like for you to give three takes of the same line, one after the other, with a little space in between so they can pick the one they like best. The implied direction is that they would like you to *change up* (*modify*) each read a little, so that they have options from which to choose their favorite. So mix it up a bit.

- "On this next one, gimme a *series*."

    This direction is also a request for multiple takes of the same line, but it implies that you just keep going until they say to stop. This might happen, for example, when you're recording efforts for a video game. You're recording *light bullet hits* (*Hunh! Aggh! Oooh!*) and they'll want a few to choose from, so they ask for a series.

- "Just gimme a couple more, *wild*."

    Often, because directors don't want to spend time slating a new take number, or maybe because they feel you're on a roll, they'll ask you for *a few more, wild*. That just means that you don't have to wait for them to slate again. They're going to keep recording. You just let 'er rip for a few more takes or until they tell you to stop.

- "Can I get a *safety*?"

    This is not a football reference. It refers to one more take for the director to have just as a backup, or maybe for another choice, or just in case the first one had a technical glitch. It usually means that your first take was fine and the director just wants an extra for good measure.

- "Gimme a little more *level* on the next pass."

    Level, in this case, refers to *audio level*, so this essentially translates to, "Louder on this next one, please."

You know who really cares about the level? The engineer.

MIC SAYS: Facing a little off-mic might save you from *blowing* the take.

THE ENGINEER

From where you'll be standing, it will, at first glance, look like the engineer's job is just to hit *record* and *stop*. Nothing could be further from the truth. Engineers are the ones who will make you sound good, and who can make it easier or harder for you to do your job; so be sure to stay on their good side. The more you work *with* them, the more pleasant your job will be.

An engineer can often fix or adjust a recorded line that would otherwise be unusable, by compressing, stretching, or adjusting levels to make the line work. Or they can ask the director to have you do it again. And again. Until you give them something useable. Treat the engineers with respect, and they're more likely to be willing to fiddle with what you've given them to make it work. Sometimes, there's nothing they can do to save a line – it's too loud, too soft, you've blown air into the mic, whatever – and you'll have to do it again anyway. Don't get impatient. Just work with them until it comes out right.

The engineer you'll be working with is only the first of several engineers who might be working on the project. But the engineer in the room, the *recording engineer*, will probably be the only one you'll see. The others will take what you've recorded and begin the lengthy editing and mixing process to distill all of your work down to the final product. That's also where sound effects and music come in, but that's for another book. Written by another author.

On rare occasions, the director and engineer will actually be the same person. This happens sometimes when a person with an engineering background gets into directing or vice versa.

An Engineer's Two Cents

Do not try to *work the mic* like a singer might do. We see a lot of music videos where a singer almost makes love to the microphone. In voice-over, it is the microphone that loves you. A VO actor must allow the engineer to bring the volume to you. You do your performance. The engineer is simply there to *capture* that performance. He is constantly working the fader to maximize every nuance that you give.

The veteran VO actors are consistent in their microphone proximity. They read to the copy – not to the mic. Newer VO actors sometimes look at the copy for most of a line and then look up at the mic at the end of the line. That changes the mic proximity, and so their sound changes.

Also, the seasoned VO actor knows what he or she sounds like and can make minor adjustments as the director demands. The highs and lows in volume within a line are in a vocal range that is acceptable range technically. Sometimes new VO actors are too dynamic – that is to say, they are too loud in the first part of a line, and then too soft in the second part. The engineer struggles to capture their performance, because there is no baseline, no sweet spot.

On *Mass Effect 2* the recording spec is: mic proximity is 12"-18" from the mic to achieve an on-camera type sound, and we use *no* compression. For an engineer, that is like working without a safety net. If we get too loud and distort, we simply do another take. That is a luxury that we try to minimize in other situations like *full cast animation* recording sessions. The trick is consistency. Whatever you establish for a character – the volume should be in a confined range.

When we get to action material, the pros also warn the engineer that it is going to get louder. That is helpful, because we are always working together to make sure we're on the same page so that your performance does not take the engineer by surprise.

Headphones: most voice actors are used to working with them, and some are not. Voice actors can be fooled by what they hear in their headphones. When an actor gets softer in volume, the engineer pushes the fader up to get more presence. The actor hears himself fine and then gets even softer. That is a problem. Some directors do not even allow headphones. They do not want the actor to *listen* to their performance because they are constantly monitoring what they hear and forget to perform as they normally would as an actor.

ELLIOT ANDERS, AUDIO ENGINEER

THE PRODUCER

The producer is in charge of making sure the project comes together just as the client or creator has imagined it. That can entail everything from hiring people to finding a studio to writing the lines you say. Producers sometimes might also be the clients, themselves, since many creators also come on as producers because of their vested interest in the project.

Producers have to make sure things stay on track from start to finish, and often they won't be in the actual session because they are handling some other aspect of the production. Remember, the recording is only one slice of the whole pie, so producers must often be master jugglers. If they don't seem to be paying attention to you, don't worry. They're probably dealing with a million other things at the moment.

As a matter of fact, if they're not paying attention to what you're doing, it's usually a good sign. It means they trust that this part of the process is going well, and they can move on to worrying about something else. If you get the chance, when you're done working, thank the producers and let them know how much you enjoyed working on their project. It's possible that they had the final say in casting you in the first place.

THE CLIENT

The client is the person or people for whom the project is being produced. They've usually hired a producer or an ad agency to take care of hiring people like the director, the recording studio, and you. Clients will only rarely be present at the recording, but will still have the final call on the end product since it is their vision (and they're paying for it!). In most projects, the final product that reaches the public will have been approved by at least the director, the producer, and finally the client.

Two good tricks to remember when dealing with the people across the glass from you:

1. Jot down their names on your script so you remember who's who.

2. If one of them gives you direction, or asks you to do something (within reason, of course), remember: don't argue with them, or explain why you did it the way you did it, or tell them why their idea sucks. Just do it. What's one more take? Right or wrong, just do it. They're the boss. Which is not to say that you should take abuse, or forget that it's your work that's going to be heard; but you must enter into this relationship with a fair amount of trust.

CHAPTER 8
YOUR HOME BOOTH

"We will either find a way, or make one."

HANNIBAL, CARTHAGINIAN
MILITARY COMMANDER

Thanks to modern technology (see *The Internet* or *Flying Cars*) you can actually set up a recording studio in your *own home*. You can do it cheap or you can do it pricey, but the power, these days, is in the hands of the people. *Psst*: that's you.

"So How Do I Set Up My Own Studio? What Do I Need?"

There are probably a million different ways you could set up your home studio, but no matter how you do it, you'll need at least four things:

1. a computer
2. a microphone
3. a computer program for audio recording
4. somewhere to record.

Odds are that you've got a computer. Perfect. One down, three to go.

Your easiest choice for a microphone is to go with something called a USB mic. You can order one on line, or you can ask for one at your local musician supply store. This mic will plug into the USB port on your computer (most computers sold in the last 15 years or so have a USB port).

Next, you need a computer program that interfaces the mic with the computer, allowing the sound going into the mic to be recorded digitally by the computer. Sometimes this program (or software) comes with your USB mic. Sometimes you already have software like this (such as Apple's *Garage Band*) installed on your computer.

If not, you can download free programs or *shareware* that will allow you to record sounds to digital files, which you can then manipulate (edit, make louder or softer, add effects). Here's a quick overview of recording software ranging from free to cheap. (Thanks to our audio guru Juan for the wisdom!)

Free

Garage Band (Mac only) is included with OSX (but even if you have to pick it up as part of iLife, it'll run you less than $100). It's easy to use, and many people are using it these days for semi-pro production. Drawbacks: set up can be confusing with some audio interfaces.

Audacity (Mac, PC, Linux) is the reigning champion of freeware audio recording software. It's compatible with all major computing platforms (even older systems) and offers an incredible collection of editing tools. Drawbacks: no true multi-tracking, and, well ... it's not the prettiest program.

WavePad (Mac & PC) is super simple and super basic, offers single track editing only, but it's a fast way to get in, record, trim, and export a piece of audio. It's also the lightest on computer resources, making it a perfect fit for older systems.

Retail

Sound Forge Pro (PC) is still one of the most comprehensive audio editing suites around. Multi-track recording has just been added, but it's designed for editing one piece of audio. Drawbacks: heavy on resources, so make sure your computer meets (preferably exceeds) Sony's system requirements for a smooth experience. It's also a little pricey for a single-track editor these days.

Pro Tools (Mac & PC) is an industry standard for a reason. If you do studio work, chances are you've encountered it. It's incredibly flexible, and is used for a variety of production environments. Drawbacks: it can be a little overwhelming for beginners, and it can be used *only* with Digidesign hardware (most commonly the Mbox), which means cost of entry is higher than many other solutions.

Honorable mentions

Reaper, Adobe Audition/Soundbooth, Logic, Sonar, GoldWave, Traverso, Acid, and *Ardour.*

Depending on how complicated you want to get, you can get interfaces like mixers and compressors in addition to the mic and the computer, but we're going to stay simple for the purposes of this book. If you want to be an audio engineer, that's a different book (one not written by us).

So you've got your equipment and your software, and you've followed the directions that came either in the box or off the Internet, and you're ready to get set up. Great. What else do you need to know? Well, even the best equipment and the best software won't help you if you don't create an environment in which you minimize external sounds. You know, like the cat, cars driving by outside, your next door neighbor who likes to sing opera at odd hours ...

We've achieved our best results in the closet. Wait a minute. That doesn't sound right. Oh, well, it's true. Got a nice walk-in closet with clothes hanging in it? Perfect. That means you won't need to put expensive acoustic foam on the walls to keep the sounds from echoing around and reducing the quality of your recording. Don't have any extra room in your closet? Find the quietest room in your house/apartment and experiment with furniture, towels, packing blankets, pillows, and other objects that might help reduce the echo in the room.

See how easy that was? You're ready to roll.

MIC SAYS: Empty egg cartons can tame echoes on the cheap.

"So What's Your Home Booth Like?"

Good question. Our home booth falls pretty much directly between cheap and expensive. We've taken all the shelves out of a hall closet and covered the walls in (some scavenged, some bought) foam. We have a decent Audio-Technica mic on a mic stand with a Popper Stopper. The mic is connected by a cable to an interface called an Mbox which is connected by a USB cable to our computer (an Apple iBook laptop). The Mbox allows us to adjust levels and listen to the recording through headphones.

We use a program called Pro Tools LE (which comes with the Mbox) to do the actual recording and editing on our computer. With the same software, we can convert a recorded audition to MP3 format (a common digital audio format that takes up little space), attach that file to an e-mail, and easily send it off to an agent or a prospective client. Total cost of our booth (minus the computer, which we already had)? About $700. We know people who have spent thousands of dollars putting their booth together and people who have spent under a $100, and all of them are working voice actors.

Setting Up a Home Booth: Man if I Had a Nickel ...

See, it's a tricky question because there is no *one* magic setup. Different voices, in different rooms, with a near infinite number of gear combinations, is enough to make even the most seasoned engineer's head spin.

Generally my advice for most folks is threefold.

1. Set a budget!

Set a dollar amount you *refuse* to go over, then *hold to it*! This stuff can get expensive *fast* (especially if you're a collector like me). This should *not* be a *max out the credit cards* budget either, but something comfortable. Some of my favorite recordings have been done on less than $250 worth of gear (minus computer of course).

2. Know your limits!

My first coaching gig had nothing to do with performance, but was with a fantastic VO actress in tears after spending thousands getting all the *right* session-grade gear: nice mic, compressor, mixer, interface, preamp. She now had a mess of knobs and cables that she was not prepared to deal with, and was very upset over not being *smart enough* to handle her own recording. I let her borrow one of my USB mics, showed her how to do some basic recording, and she booked her first gig from home a week later.

3. Give it time!

And I don't mean time sitting around collecting dust, I mean time using this gear *every day*! Just because setting up a USB mic is easy (uh ... plug it in?) doesn't mean you will know how to record competitive auditions. Don't start sending out audio right away. Practice with it *a lot* first. After you're feeling pretty comfy, once you can set up, record, edit, and send without having to think out each step, *then* send some samples out to qualified individuals for some feedback (preferably us engineers, but agents and other VO talent can help too).

You won't need to get a degree in audio production, but you *will* need to learn a little about how recording works, a *very* little, as most recording programs now use commands similar to word processors (drag to select, cut, copy, paste, make font/volume bigger or smaller, etc).

Who knows? You might just find you like your time behind the mixer as much as your time behind the mic ...

JUAN C. BAGNELL,
DIRECTOR, AUDIO ENGINEER

CHANGING TECHNOLOGY AND THE FUTURE OF VO

Since technology changes at the speed of ... technology, it's important to remember that even as you're reading this now, somewhere, someone is developing something to make things run faster, better, and cheaper. A good bit of advice, whatever your career, is do your homework and research technology related to your industry (in this case, VO).

If you need to buy a microphone, for example, jump on the Internet, or drive down to your local audio equipment store and ask around. Check out what has just come on the market, and see if it has the capabilities that you need to do what you want. Sometimes it's better to go with a time-tested device that's already had all the bugs worked out, while other times it can be fun to be the first kid on your block with a new toy. Either way, do your research. In today's world, with information so readily available, there's no excuse to do otherwise.

Is it time for you to build the perfect home studio now? Well, the beauty of it all is that you can start small and upgrade at your own pace. If you're just starting out and basically messing around to get used to recording VO, don't spend a lot of money. Get a cheap USB mic, plug it into your computer, and away you go!

Then maybe you'll get to a point where you want to be recording auditions and sending them out. Make sure you've created a relatively soundproof place to record in. Maybe get a better mic and download some free sound-editing software. Wanna start recording your own projects and really getting into some serious editing? Invest in a really good mic and buy the equipment that you need.

Think about it: just a few years ago, almost no one had a home recording studio. Equipment was too expensive, and what could you really achieve at home anyway? Then suddenly, as things started moving more quickly in the industry (thanks in part to the Internet), actors realized they could get a jump on things by recording themselves at home and sending their auditions directly to the people who were in charge of hiring. Computers became cheaper and so did audio equipment.

Now, most of the VAs we know have home studios, or at least professional recording equipment of a certain caliber and a space to record with good clean sound. And the market follows suit. At least one of Los Angeles's largest voice-over agencies now insists that its clients record all their auditions from home rather than coming into the agency to record them.

Of course, some argue that, with technology advancing as fast as it is, soon there may be hardly any need for live voice-over actors. Look at how skillfully computer generated imaging (CGI) is replicating the human form in films today, for example.

We choose to believe differently, preferring the argument that there will always be some things that humans will do better than computers, and that voice acting is one of those things. That is another reason your skill as an actor will serve you in this business, regardless of changes in the technology itself.

CHAPTER 9
WHAT TO DO TO GET STARTED

"Everyone who got where he is has had to begin where he was."

ROBERT LOUIS STEVENSON, SCOTTISH NOVELIST

BE PREPARED: THE WAY OF THE BOY SCOUT

"So what's the next step?" you might be asking yourself. "I'm thirteen, I'm still in school, I live in Wichita Kansas," you say. "I'm an on-camera actor living in Los Angeles who's looking for another source of income where I still get to act." Or, "I'm forty, I'm married, I work eight hours a day in an office."

Have no fear, no matter what your situation, there are things you can do. If you've read this far, then you already have a pretty good idea of what kinds of voice-over jobs are out there, the type of work each entails, and generally how things work and who you're dealing with. So how can you take that information and translate it into a wildly successful career in the voice-over industry?

Well, we've said it before, and we'll lay down the caveat once more for good measure: as with any art or creative industry, the path to success is not a straight one in this business. Nor does it come with a map. You can be phenomenally talented and still have to work hard. You may work hard for a year or for ten years before you feel you've *made it*. So make sure you're having fun. The only things you can truly do (besides having fun) to create the best odds of succeeding are to get prepared and stay prepared, so that when the opportunities that you create pop up, you can take full advantage of them.

Luck

They say that luck plays a huge part in getting anywhere in this business: "Ya just gotta be at the right place at the right time!" We agree, but we also have a slightly different definition of *luck*. Our friend Merriam – you may know her: *Merriam-Webster* – defines luck as:

> 1. (a) a force that brings good fortune or adversity (b) the events or circumstances that operate for or against an individual

We don't like that definition because it makes it seem as if we have no control whatsoever over getting what we want: if the mystical force that is luck is feeling *off* that day, we're screwed. The mid-1st century Roman philosopher Seneca said, "Luck is what happens when preparation meets opportunity," and that's how we'd rather look at it.

To take this a step further, instead of *luck*, we prefer to substitute the word *success* in Seneca's definition. We end up with the equation: *success = preparation + opportunity*. This is much better than relying on luck because you can take action to prepare yourself, and you can take action to create opportunities.

We do our best to be prepared and to create our own opportunities, and that's when we've found success happens most often for us. So what they say *is* true: luck plays a bit part. But you can get yourself to the right place, and if it's the right time and you're prepared, then boom!

But imagine what happens if you manage to get to the right place at the right time and you're *not* ready for it: the, uh... opposite of boom.

MIC SAYS: ~~Luck~~ Success = Preparation + Opportunity

READ MUCH?

For some people, reading aloud can be a scary thing. To make it as a voice actor, you'll have to overcome that fear. Take a class in reading comprehension to hone your verbal skills so that you're more comfortable. If you have dyslexia or a medical issue that makes reading difficult, do whatever it takes to increase your confidence when reading.

You could have someone read the copy or script into a recorder and work with it that way, memorizing it as best you can. But this will limit the types of jobs you'll be able to work on, since some types of voice-over are so fast-paced, and the script changes so frequently, that there often isn't time to have someone record things for you in advance. We do know an actor who is legally blind, but is still a successful working voice actor because he's figured out a system that works for him; so nothing is impossible. Just examine your strengths and weaknesses, and take steps to exploit and improve them wherever you can.

Here's an exercise you can try while reading out loud: take only a quick look at the following sentence, then look up from the book and try saying it aloud from memory:

Hey there, Bob. I thought I heard you come in. Your coffee and paper are on the table.

Were you able to remember the line? Did you leave out a word? Try it again. How about this time? Better?

You can do this exercise while reading anything. *Pulling the lines off the page* like this is a skill that'll come in quite handy. This is especially true in dubbing, where you have to watch the screen to match the character's lip flaps. But it'll also be helpful when recording pre-lay animation, allowing you to make eye contact with the other actors while you're reading.

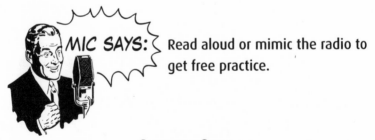

MIC SAYS: Read aloud or mimic the radio to get free practice.

START SMALL

We've given you a lot of things to think about, and it can easily become overwhelming deciding what to do first. You don't have to move to Los Angeles, get into a class, and record a demo today. Start with one small thing, and when you feel that you've accomplished that or have comfortably worked it into your routine, add another thing. Nothing'll crush your spirit harder, and paralyze you faster, than thinking you have to do it all at once.

Make a list. Pick one action that sounds fun (you'll be more inclined to do it that way), and start there.

You can begin with something as small as warming up your voice in the shower, or reading a news article aloud, or making sure you drink two extra glasses of water that day.

There's a saying: "What you practice every day is what you will become." And what's the best way to stay on target with your practice? Create a routine.

YOUR ROUTINE

Creating a routine helps you actually *do* things. Plan out a time every day or every couple of days for working on something specific, even for just fifteen minutes at a time. In addition to whatever you may choose to work on, there are practice scripts at the end of this book for your study and pleasure. But also see what you can find on your own.

Troll the Internet for scripts and advertising that you can pull, or go through magazines and tear out interesting ads. Put together a book of your own practice copy, and take it out from time to time when you want to exercise your skills. Or better yet, get some friends together and record each other reading, then listen to the playback and talk about what you sound like.

One of the best ways to grow is to take a look at what you're doing and learn from it: what you like about it, what seems to work, and what you can experiment with in the future. Practice dubbing your favorite show (not for sale or public viewing, of course; we're not endorsing anything illegal here).

Watch cartoons and mimic the voices you hear. *Come on! How many study plans ask you to watch cartoons? Isn't this great?* Practice doing the work you want to be doing so that your body and mind start to get used to your new skill, and then get better at it. Record yourself and listen to the playback so that you know what other people are hearing when you speak. And *don't be judgmental.*

If you find (or already know) that you have an actual speech impediment, say a lisp, for example, don't give up right away. There are two obvious paths open to you:

1. Embrace it. Many people have become famous *because* of their impediment. However, know that this will limit you as a voice actor, because you might get cast only as characters for which a lisp works.

2. The better path (in our humble opinion) is to find a speech therapist to help you overcome the impediment. Sometimes this therapy is offered by schools for free. Yuri used to have a lisp when he was younger, but has since corrected it through speech therapy classes that were offered at his school. Eliminating his lisp has definitely opened up the number of roles that he's eligible for.

The same goes for accents. If you have an accent, use it to your advantage whenever possible. But to avoid limiting the types of roles that you'll end up playing, make sure you can also read and speak in whatever dialect rules where you're working.

Let part of your routine include a physical and vocal warm-up. Warming up your body will not only put you into a ready physical state for working, but can ultimately become part of your ritual to prepare yourself for auditions or jobs. To get you started, we have included several warm-ups in Chapter 4, *Before You Get to the Audition.* But whatever you do, create a warm-up routine that works for *you.*

The radio is your friend

Listen to the radio and start mimicking what you hear. Pay attention to the vocal qualities or attitudes of the actors who have been hired to sell products. You'll hear all types, from newscasters to DJs to commercial actors to public service announcers.

Use this free (did we mention *free?*) resource to begin to recognize who's out there and what they're getting hired to sell. We noted earlier that *hot* vocal qualities change with the times. You'll want to stay up to date with what's really going on out there. If everything you are hearing on the radio happens to be *wry* or *matter of fact*, perhaps think about strengthening those qualities in your own repertoire.

The same goes for TV. Watch it. Listen. And learn.

Get your mouth moving

Practice reading aloud because, trust us, you're going to be doing a lot of it. Get your favorite book, magazine, or whatever's lying on the coffee table, and start reading out loud. Just get your mouth accustomed to reading and vocalizing.

Try different types of material (newspaper articles, short stories, children's books, advertisements) so that you get comfortable with any type of VO copy that may come your way. If you're waiting at the bus stop, pick up that pamphlet on the bench next to you and start reading, or take a stab at the poster on the wall next to you. Get your mouth and mind used to reading unfamiliar material and making sense of it on the fly.

CLASSES, CLASSES, CLASSES

Get into a *voice class* (for singing, breath, voice-over, or vocal placement). Classes will help you learn as much as you can about yourself and your voice. Each of these different classes will, no doubt, have something unique to offer. So make sure you research a class before you commit, to see what you should expect. Get recommendations from people you trust who have taken classes you are interested in. Just putting yourself in a situation in which you get to work on your craft with other like-minded individuals often can lead you to wonderful things.

Easy as 1-2-3

I got into voice-over completely by accident. I didn't take a class until I'd appeared in several episodes of original animated series and done a few recurring/regular roles on anime series, a handful of video games, and more than a few radio commercials. The class I took *should* have been taken at the beginning of my work in VO.

Example: I went in to record a series of radio commercials for a theme park in Salt Lake City, and the engineer said to me, "This take, give me an 'ABC,'" which means to do three different takes of the same line. But I didn't know that.

So, he told me we were rolling and slated me. When he pointed at me to record, I proudly said, without missing a beat: "A, B, C."

A huge laugh came from the control room, the phone patched producers, and the actors in the booth with me. Ahhh, yes. Another lesson learned ... the *hard* way.

HENRY DITTMAN, ACTOR

THAT SHINY, HAPPY THING
WE CALL THE DEMO

If you're serious about this whole voice acting thing, one item you'll need eventually is a sample of your voice and your acting: your *demo*. On-camera and theatre actors, to put themselves out there professionally, need a picture and résumé. Voice actors need a demo, which is sometimes also called a *reel*.

Some voice-over classes actually offer demo production as a part of their curriculum, and some classes are even dedicated purely to creating a demo. Remember, this will be your calling card in the beginning, your *first impression* on many of the people who could potentially hire you. As with all first impressions, you want your reel to be as good as it can be. So don't rush to throw just anything together. You don't want your demo to sound cheap or unprofessional.

That means you're going to want to spend a little money on it. The best demos have a variety of sounds and styles on them, but are also succinct and clear, as well as professionally produced and mixed. More on creating your demo in the very next chapter: Chapter 10, *The Demo.*

STAYING PREPARED

We've covered some of the ways you can prepare yourself for work as a voice actor, but how do you *stay* prepared?

Getting prepared involves breaking out of your comfort zone, learning new and exciting things, and strengthening muscles you didn't even know were there. Staying prepared is like keeping your engine revving after all that preparation, so that when the starter's pistol goes off, you're ready to go. Really, what would be the point of spending time, money, and energy on classes, or a demo, or your routine, if you're going to stop making an effort the minute the class, activity, or job is done? We mean, *really.*

Just as an athlete plays practice games in preparation for a competition, or a doctor or lawyer attends continuing education classes to stay on top of the latest developments in his or her field, your job as an actor is do what it takes so that you are always ready for the job or audition around the corner. You hope an opportunity happens soon and comes often, but you never really know when an audition or job is going to pounce. That means you need to stay warmed up so that when it does, you're ready. Get into an acting class that is ongoing; do a play from time to time. Something, anything, that'll keep your creative acting juices flowing.

Stick to the routine you've developed. Continue to do warm-ups just as you did to strengthen and train your voice in the first place. Maybe change up your routine here and there to keep it from getting boring. And interact with others who might be doing the same thing you're doing. Social networking has become invaluable to this profession, and the Internet (have we mentioned how much we love the World Wide Web?) has made it much easier for you to access information. Often, your best teachers are the people you encounter in your everyday life.

Make sure you are treating your voice right. If you do find yourself in situations that may be unhealthy for your voice – screaming at a concert, lack of sleep followed by a ton of caffeine to compensate, hanging out in smoky clubs – then do things that you know will help get your voice back on track. Hum to get your vocal cords lubricated and warmed up; give yourself a self-imposed vocal rest if you need it. (It is said that actor and comedian John Leguizamo will often maintain long periods of silence while working on challenging vocal performances, simply to keep his vocal cords in a state of readiness).

There are many schools of thought as to what may affect the health of your voice for better or for worse. Suffice to say, different things work for different people in different situations, so experiment a bit and see what works for *you*.

READY, SET...GO! (NO, SERIOUSLY, GO)

If you've done all the things you can wherever it is you live, and you still find yourself in love with acting, and you're chomping at the bit, hie thee to where the work is (especially if you're far removed from a major voice-over hub).

Yes, in theory, VO can be done from anywhere there's a recording booth. But we've learned that a lot of places want you to come in and audition live for them; and if you get the job, they might want you in the studio later that same day or at nine o'clock the next morning. You know how expensive plane tickets are if you buy them the day of the flight? Whatever they cost, we're betting it's more than what you're going to make doing the job under most circumstances.

And think about it for a second: with millions of people in the world who call themselves actors, what would happen if a job was open to all of them at the same time? The casting people wouldn't have enough time to listen to all of the submissions. So for the CDs, it's far easier to limit the pool they're choosing from – and that's where you want to be swimming. Dive into that pool. Go where the work is.

THE BIG DUB-OUT

It was another hot, sweltering, summer day in 2001. It was already 10 a.m., so we dressed quickly and dragged ourselves downstairs to the second floor of the hotel, only to discover we had missed breakfast once again. I needed coffee, *bad*. So, we hustled across the street to our local neighborhood deli. I had been there the night before, and enjoyed the similarities to a Smilers in NYC, or a 7-Eleven in L.A. Only, this was Italy. No, not Little Italy. Rome, Italy. Ya know, the country shaped like a boot in the Mediterranean Sea? And I was far from my home in Hollywood, CA.

Hello, I said, *Hello*, with no response from the guys behind the counter. *Hello-oo, Ciao, Buon giorno, Hello-oo?* Over the glass, I saw two very hot, young, Italian hunks. They were both, tall, dark, and very handsome. *Hello, Helloo-oo* they called back at me, playing with their vocal tones, trying to copy my voice with their *hellos*. Laughing, I said *hello* back, and then we all started laughing. *Hello, Hello-oo, Hello-oo* ... all of us just laughing away.

"Do you know what she does for a living?" my friend asked with a mischievous smile. "She is on *Digimon!*"

All of a sudden, the Italians came from behind the glass counter, repeating, *Digimon, Digimon, Digimon!* They kept saying it, like a mantra, as another Italian hunk came out from the back. *Digimon, Digimon, Digimon.* Each of the three hunks kissed me on both cheeks (did I say how much I love Italy?), and had me chant with them. *Digimon, Digimon, Digimon.* The Italians were thrilled to discover a Hollywood animation star, right in their little deli. They all knew the series and wouldn't let me pay for my grub. I felt pretty good drinking that hot coffee. Ah, the perks of celebrity.

Later that day, I went to the largest flea market in Rome. It was gigantic, the biggest flea market I had ever seen. I started going down the aisles, one by one. On one of the long tables, I spotted "Patamon," the character I voiced on *Digimon.* Oh wow, my first talking toy of a character I created, right here in Italy. While out of the country, I had gone "International." Isn't show business grand? I was thrilled and quickly bought my first "Patamon" (who desperately needed batteries).

It was a hot, sweltering day. As I unpacked my suitcase, I finally got the opportunity to check out "Patamon" in his Hollywood home. I opened up the little guy, and noticed he was made in China. Carefully, I put the batteries in. I pressed the button and listened intently as this little voice said, "Bueno, bueno, bueno." Oh wow, oh wow, it wasn't me ... My voice had been dubbed ... in Italian.

LAURA SUMMER, ACTRESS

Top VO Cities

It doesn't matter where you live. No matter what country you call home, there are likely to be certain cities where the entertainment industry – VO in particular – congregates. In most countries, the larger cities offer more work. For example Paris, France; London, England; and Vancouver, Toronto, and Montreal, Canada, all have thriving communities of working voice actors.

In the U.S. (where we're most familiar with things) there are several hot spots. The major U.S. hubs for VO work seem to be:

1. Los Angeles, CA
2. New York, NY
3. Dallas, TX
4. Chicago, IL
5. Nashville, TN
6. Atlanta, GA

There are other cities in which voice-over is recorded, and they can be a great training ground as you begin. But to really be in the thick of it and have the best opportunity to make a living at VO, it is best to locate yourself in one of the major cities. We're based in L.A. and have found some measure of success here, and we have friends in other cities who are also doing quite well in their respective markets.

Sometimes, when a voice actor achieves a certain level of success, he or she can move away from the hustle and bustle of the top cities and let the work come to him or her. We worked with a well-known actor who lives in Kansas City and records everything from home, coming into L.A. only on very rare occasions to put in face time. But remember, you'll have to establish yourself first. So get in the game!

CHAPTER 10
THE DEMO

"Empty pockets never held anyone back. Only empty heads
and empty hearts can do that."

NORMAN VINCENT PEALE,
U.S. MOTIVATIONAL SPEAKER, AUTHOR, MINISTER

YOUR CALLING C[AR]D...

A s promised, we've arrived at the *demo*, or demonstration, of
you and your many talents. It's not enough to record yourself
just doing all the crazy voices and impressions you can do into a
tape recorder (or even into *Garage Band*, as the kids are calling it
these days). You need a demo that will be competitive in order to
open the right doors and get you noticed by the right people. And
this means that, as tempting as it may be to get your second-cousin-
twice-removed-the-wedding-DJ to record you in his garage, you
might want to consider getting your demo professionally produced.

It is, after all, going to be the professional world's first impression of you and what you have to offer. You don't want to give them any excuses not to fall in love with you.

Your demo reel can be geared specifically toward a particular area of VO work. For example, actors who focus primarily on commercial work don't always have an animation demo. Promo or narration folks sometimes stick to their areas of expertise and have a demo that showcases only their talent for that kind of work. Some people have a different demo for each type of VO, while others just split their one demo into separate tracks that highlight the different areas. Your demo can be as specific or diverse as you want. The most important thing is to do it well.

FAKE IT 'TIL YOU MAKE IT

"But I haven't done any work yet! What am I supposed to put on my reel?" you may ask, your brow furrowing in panic and dismay. Relax that brow. A demo reel doesn't have to be from actual work you have already done; more often than not, everything on a demo is totally fabricated. As a matter of fact, even if you do have some real material to put on your reel, you may want to put made-up stuff on it anyway. This will allow you to focus the demo and highlight the qualities that you want to showcase. After all, *demo* can also mean *demonstration* of what you *can* do, not necessarily what you *have* done.

Now here's a thing that's going to highlight the weirdness of the entertainment biz: all agents know that actors make up most of what's on their demos, especially when just starting out; but they still want to be fooled. So that's what you've gotta do. Fool 'em as best you can. Let's see how you can do that.

What are you going to record? Well, first we're going to

caution you against copying things directly from other commercial spots you hear or shows you see. The reason for that is this: as big as you think this world is, people are paying attention; and with people like casting directors and agents, it's *their job* to pay attention.

You don't want to record yourself doing a McDonald's spot you heard on the radio or shouting out the catchphrase of a popular animated character, and then send it to an agency whose client actually *did* record that spot or character. Your demo will immediately be outed and possibly thrown away. That's not to say it's definitely going to happen, but we feel that in this situation, it's better to be safe than sorry, especially when there are easy ways to cover your tracks.

This seems like a good place to mention something else that we feel is important and will serve you throughout your long career in this business: *don't lie about the work you've done.* There might be a temptation to say that you worked on things you didn't work on so you seem more experienced to a possible employer, especially in the beginning when you don't have any credits to speak of. *Don't.* Don't do it.

We're not saying you should open every conversation with, "Okay, now, I just want you to know that I have never done this before." If they don't ask, let 'em think what they want. But don't put titles that you didn't work on, on your résumé because you'll be working in a very tight circle of people. And if the person reading your résumé didn't cast it, odds are he or she knows the person who did, or the director; and being caught in a lie is a great way to get remembered for all the wrong reasons. Don't get caught up in trying to make people think you're much more experienced than you are. If they like you, they're going to want to be the one who *discovered* you. Let 'em discover you.

After reading the last few paragraphs, you may be saying to yourself, "Hey, first they're telling me to fake it and now they're telling me not to lie. What gives?" Sure, our advice on these two issues can be seen as inconsistent, but trust us on this one. Acting is a business of illusion, and the demo is an accepted bending of the rules in this world. Taking credit for things you did not do, not so much.

Now that we've hopefully made that clear, let's get back to making your demo sound as legit as you can. "But if I can't copy real things, how am I supposed to know what to record?" you may ask. Well, here's another place where we're going to ask you to employ that powerful imagination of yours. Look at some real stuff … and then mess with it.

To create commercial copy for your reel, go pick up a magazine and flip through the ads. Print ads are written differently than radio or TV ads, so you won't ever have to worry about someone already having recorded this spot. Now mess with it, rewrite it a bit, and make it your own.

Do the same for animation and video game bits. Watch, listen, play, take notes. Then mess with it, riff on it, make it your own. If you really hate writing, find a friend who's good at it and see if he or she will help you. Before you know it, you'll have scripts to record. And you don't need many.

Let's say you've recorded your demo as professionally as you can. Now, you'll want someone (an audio engineer) to spend time mixing it and *sweetening* it with effects and music, so that it sounds as if the spots were pulled from actual shows or commercials. The engineer will work with each clip you've recorded as if it were a real spot, and make it sound as good as possible; then you'll work together to pull your favorite section of each spot.

You'll want your demo to run about sixty seconds total, so

you'll have to pick only the best part from each spot. Agents and casting directors are busy people. They're not going to have time to listen to a five-minute demo, so you gotta hook 'em quickly and leave 'em wanting more.

Another trick that engineers often use to help the demo reel sound more *realistic* is to change the recording levels and settings between the different spots. This way, even if you record them back-to-back in one session, the sound quality will be slightly different from spot to spot, just as if you had recorded each spot at a different time in a different studio with a different engineer. You can even help the engineer achieve this effect by changing your position slightly from script to script. It may seem funny, but sound is a finicky thing; and little things, even moving an inch back from the mic, or an inch left or right, can drastically affect how your voice is recorded. That's why, if you record at a certain studio regularly, you may notice the mic setup is always the same in order to maintain consistency in recording.

All of these things will add up to a professional sounding demo, which will be key in helping to open the doors that lead to work. Don't be afraid to spend both time and money on your demo, but also don't be afraid to shop around. If a deal seems too good to be true, make sure it isn't by first doing a little research on your own. If the Internet's good for something, it's research. Well, research and downloading videos of cats doing cute things.

MAKING IT YOUR OWN

When I first had aspirations of becoming a voice actor in college, I paid a voice-over teacher to coach me and help make my demo. We worked through different voices she felt would be good, and pulled bits from a stack of copy she had. Years later, when I became a producer and had to cast a few shows, I was surprised to hear other actors with some of the *same* bits of copy on their demos. It was embarrassing. That's why I encourage people to write their own stuff for their demos. That way it will be guaranteed to be original, and you'll never have to worry that any agent, producer, or casting director has heard that same bit over and over again.

— STEPHANIE SHEH,
ACTRESS, DIRECTOR, WRITER

PLAY TO YOUR STRENGTHS

We talked earlier about *finding your voice* and the adjectives that best describe it, and suggested making a quality list. This is particularly important when creating your demo. To market and promote yourself most successfully, you'll want to be comfortable with and aware of the strengths and weaknesses of your voice. As you plan and execute your demo, knowing these attributes will help you zero in on what will best showcase you.

Let's narrow it down a bit. Using the list below, see which adjectives best describe the main qualities of your voice. Think honestly about which ones would be a stretch and which ones are right in your wheelhouse. Also, for your own reference, see if you feel any of these qualities describe a trend you are currently hearing on TV or radio. If you think of adjectives that are not on this list, add them. This is not the be-all end-all list of adjectives.

wry	calm	perky
honest	open	cut-to-the-chase
sarcastic	happy	clipped
giddy	haughty	innocent
secretive	emotional	bored

MIC SAYS: Leading your demo with your strongest voice ensures that even listeners with short attention spans will hear you at your best.

THE COMMERCIAL DEMO

We've already noted that there are several different types of demos. Let's start our discussion with the commercial demo.

A solid commercial demo usually has a mix of several kinds of spots: a hard sell, a soft sell, a partner-read/dialogue spot, a PSA, an upscale sell, a legal disclaimer, and sometimes a character spot. You already know that you have about sixty seconds to cover these spots on your reel.

There is no absolute order in which the different spots should be placed on the reel, and no rule about whether you need to include every kind of read. Just try to keep the sounds different from spot to spot. In other words, if your upscale sell has a similar vibe to your soft sell, break them up by putting one of the other spots in between. Also remember that the people listening to your demo may have very short attention spans, so put a couple of your strongest reads in first and second position. If you have only fifteen seconds to grab them, make sure you're really showing them who you are.

But don't load your demo up with different examples of one *type* of spot, even if you believe that it's what you do best. Having a good mix on your demo will show that you're proficient in an array of different types of copy. Let them know that you'll be able to handle anything that gets thrown at you in the booth.

The *hard sell* or sometimes, *high energy* sell, is just what it sounds like: a forceful and direct attempt to convince a consumer to buy a product. You've heard this type of spot before: *You need this! Buy now, while supplies last! Be the first one on the block to own one! We're almost giving them away!*

There's been a noticeable decline of the hard sell, but it's still out there. You'll notice it a lot in ads that are selling to kids. Check out the ads for cereal and toys in between cartoons on Saturday morning.

A *soft sell* spot is essentially the opposite of the hard sell. The soft sell is a more subtle approach, giving potential customers just enough indirect information to get them to come to the conclusion themselves that they need to buy whatever it is you're selling. Often these spots use comedy to get you feeling good, and then associate the product with the good feeling you're experiencing. Your brain does the rest: "Ha ha ha! ... I feel good ... Maybe if I get this product, it'll make me feel good!"

The soft sell will likely be less energetic than the hard sell, and more natural and friendly – stressing the personal, intimate connection with listeners rather than trying to convince them to buy something.

For the *partner read* (also called a *dialogue spot*), the material can be either high energy or low energy. What is most important is to have at least two distinct voices (you and another actor) talking to one another. In the partner read, you two will be discussing something and joking, arguing, or learning about the product. This spot will help add texture to your demo by having someone else's voice bring contrast to your own. Always try to get someone of the opposite sex to record this spot with you; we don't want the listener to become confused as to whose demo they're listening to. Doing a dialogue spot for your demo can be a great way to collaborate with a friend who is also interested in VO and may be able to use the spot on his or her reel as well!

A *PSA*, or *Public Service Announcement*, is a little different. We're sure you've heard many PSAs. They are primarily geared towards causing a strong emotional reaction in the listener, and most often promote issues of health and safety. Common PSA topics are anti drug use, pro seatbelt use, and support for charitable causes. They can be shocking, bring tears to your eyes by uplifting you, or make you feel sad and wistful: *One out of every six children is diagnosed with a learning disability* ... The vocal quality of these spots is generally low energy and intimate, sometimes no louder than a whisper.

The *upscale read* is often referred to as a *perfume* or *car sell*, and we sometimes like to call it the *sexy voice*. This read is most often used to sell luxury products geared toward a very elite crowd, and positively drips with wealth and comfort. It says, *Hey, I'm part of this secret club and you're part of this secret club. We both know what's best, don't we? And if you're not a member yet, buy one of these, and I'll pull you out of the riffraff.*

We say it's *sexy* because upscale spots tend to have either a sultry female voice or a male voice cooing and purring seductively about the product. The implication is that the product will bring you wealth, power, and sex. It's kind of a cross between the hard and soft sells when it comes to the approach, but the delivery is soft, intimate, and sensual. If you're younger, or have a younger sounding voice, you might consider leaving this read off your demo. A younger voice trying to sound adult and sexy may just end up making the listener feel uncomfortable ... and that's not what we're trying to do here.

The *legal disclaimer* (sometimes referred to as just *the legal*) is also kind of optional on your demo, but it doesn't take up much time and does come up a lot in commercials. It can also be fun, so give it a try and see what happens. The legal is that bit at the end of the spot that often ends with *Prices and participation may vary*, and that goes by so fast, you almost can't tell what's being said. This is done intentionally, partly because they'd rather not draw your attention to the legal jargon, but also because there is only so much time to cram everything into the commercial. Some people are really, *really* good at this, so if you're not, no worries.

Whatever you do, don't have an engineer speed up your voice to sound faster. Even if you fool people on your demo, one day you'll get asked to do it for real, and then you'll be in a pickle. Pay attention to the legal next time you're listening to a commercial. (Usually you'll hear it on radio spots because in TV spots the legal can be flashed on screen in small print near the bottom.) Listen to the actor's delivery. Try and repeat it. Heck, try and say, *Prices and participation may vary*, three times – *fast*. It's not easy.

And finally the character spot. The *character spot* is one with which you might get to play a little more while creating your commercial demo. This is *not* your average girl/guy-next-door read: you may be using a totally unique delivery to characterize a talking lemon, or a squirrel, or a robot.* Have fun. The character spot might be a great place to showcase your dialects or an oddball voice that wouldn't fit into any of the other spots. If you haven't had an opportunity yet on your demo to show off something fun that you can do well, this may be the place.

*This is not to say that any of these characters wouldn't be just as interesting in your own normal voice. And if you actually *are* a talking lemon, a squirrel, or a robot, the authors apologize for this apparent discrimination.

THE PROMO DEMO

Promos are similar to commercials but have their own specific feel, and some people have made entire careers in promo VO. Remember, promo is short for *promotional*, so you're going to be promoting something. What's a promo sound like? Well, movie trailers are good examples of promos: *In a world ... where a person's voice is the only weapon he has ... one man must defy all odds to become the ultimate warrior ...*

Of course doing VO for movie trailers is highly coveted work and hard to come by. But there's other promo work out there, such as the ads you hear promoting different networks or programs: *Tonight on FOX! You'll never believe the trouble Tara's gotten herself into this time, on TV's hottest new reality show,* Tara Uncensored! *Tonight at 9!*

Promos can be found on television, the Internet, airplanes, and even cell phones.

The *promo voice* was traditionally a very specific official-sounding voice, but as times have changed, so have promos. On a network like E! you may hear a very high-energy promo voice which is very different than the low, dramatic quality of the typical movie trailer delivery.

A promo reel needs to have a variety of examples. Listen to some different promos to see where your strengths may lie before creating your own (not everyone can be the movie trailer guy). Perhaps you'll hear a trailer for your favorite TV show, announcements for an awards show, or even the voice of a company when you visit its Web site. Your promo reel might have spots of differing lengths since some promos can be quite short while others are much longer. Feel free to mix it up a little, but keep in mind that you don't want the listener to get too much of any one thing.

In general, the rule for any demo is *shorter is better*. Agents and casting directors will thank you for it.

THE ANIMATION/VIDEO GAME DEMO

Once just a humble animation reel, now it's called an animation/video game reel. Obviously, we have a special place in our hearts for animation and video games. For this reel you should really feel free to let yourself play. However, as we've mentioned before, it's not just about coming up with crazy cartoon voices. Lead with your strengths, as in other reels, and make sure you include some characters that sound like you without *putting on* a voice.

There are a lot of *normal* characters in video games and animation. Soldiers, spies, doctors, and princes can live in the same world as dragons, dwarves, and aliens. Just make sure that you put them in interesting situations when you're writing words for them.

If you are better at some voices than others, make sure you use longer clips of the best ones. Don't feel as if you have to include every voice under the sun on your reel. Pick your best.

If you want to showcase dialects, this is the place to do it. But make sure you're *really* good at the dialects you lay down. If you need to, practice with a dialect coach before recording your demo. Nothing turns an agent or casting director off faster than a poor, or even mediocre, dialect.

All animation clips you create should, of course, be sweetened with effects and music to sound as real as possible.

And once again, try to remember that those listening to your reel don't need to hear an entire show or even a full scene. They simply want to hear enough to tell two things:

1. What do you sound like?
2. Can you act?

If you're incredibly versatile – a man or woman (or robot) of a thousand voices – that's great, a bonus. But first establish the two things most cared about: your sound and your acting skill. Only then should you go for what's in your back pocket. You don't even necessarily have to use complete sentences: feel free to cut things in the middle. It is always better to leave people wanting more than to give them enough to get tired of.

The animation section of a demo can be a wonderful opportunity for you to create fun copy for yourself. Think about the kinds of characters you'd love to be playing. Now you get to create them, tailor them to exactly what you want, what you like. Cast yourself! How empowering is that!?

Also consider whether or not you need an additional actor to read some dialogue opposite you in a scene. If you say, "I'll get you," and, "Oh, yes I will," wouldn't it be fun to have someone interject, "No, you won't," between your lines to add more depth and realism to the interaction? Remember, don't pick someone whose vocal print is close to yours; someone of the opposite sex might be best. After all, we don't want the listener falling in love with your *partner's* voice.

With your animation/video game demo in particular, make sure to include action in some of your clips. There's a lot of fighting and jumping around in cartoons and video games, and these days, directors are asking for movie-like realism. As a matter of fact, to put the actors in the right frame of mind in one VG recording session, the director actually had the actors listen to battle scenes from the movie *Black Hawk Down* in their headphones while recording. Show them you can throw down in the booth. Give them a little laughing, a little yelling over gunfire, a little getting hit in the gut. No animation is complete without these sounds. Creating believable efforts is a valuable skill, and if you're good at it, people will remember you. Trust us.

THE NARRATION DEMO

The final type of demo we want to go over is the narration demo. Narration can be for fiction or non-fiction material, for film, TV, or audiobooks. Because of that, we recommend mixing it up a bit on your reel. Throw in a little narration for a documentary or nature special: *The mother polar bear is particularly protective of her cubs, but as you can see, they can be quite a handful* ... But also include a little narration from a children's animated movie or a fantasy epic: *Once upon a time, in the land of McMukmuk, two churlish dwarves began a quest that would not only test their skills, but their friendship* ...

There is a cornucopia of styles to choose from: history books, children's books, medical or legal tomes, and many more. Try some plainer texts, and then if you feel adventurous, move to stories that will require you to play a variety of different characters. On the other hand, if you find that your voice (and you) tend toward a specific type of narration, don't be afraid to focus on that in your reel.

These clips are expected to be a little longer than others because it's going to be important that the listener hear you maintain a tone and pace over time. Still, a few sentences or even a short paragraph per sample should be plenty. And for the narration demo, don't feel compelled to create your own material. Feel free to read aloud from not only different genre books, but anything from self-help to textbooks and technical writings.

You might also try children's books and classical literature to give your demo a nice variety. This is easier than having to write something yourself, and you can get all your material for free at your local library.

Make sure that with any copy you read, you know the correct way to pronounce every word, especially if the copy is technical, medical, or full of tough words. If you're unsure, find something else to read. You don't want to sound unqualified or unprofessional simply because you don't know how to pronounce something correctly. With narration, especially for non-fiction, it is absolutely crucial that you sound like you know what you are talking about. Even if you don't.

MAKING YOUR DEMO: COSTLY, BUT WORTH IT

Taking classes on demo-making and creating the demo itself can become quite costly, so make sure you understand all the hidden costs as well as the up-front costs. Do you have to pay the director for his or her time, as well as the engineer, as well as the recording studio? What about the time the engineer has to spend sweetening your demo after you're are done recording in the booth? You will also have to make copies of your demo and possibly design (or have someone design) labels. Then there are the mailings to get your demos into the hands of agents, studios, and casting people.

From the start, research and list these costs to cut down on unwelcome surprises along the way. Make sure you have enough funding to get the job done. Start a savings account (or a glass jar) today for your demo production, and commit to putting a few dollars a week into it. How about $10-$20? By the time you're done preparing for your demo, you'll have the money to pay for it.

So how much is it gonna cost? You need to know that before you start. Depending on where you're located and who you know, you can count on spending anywhere from $500 to $2000 on a good demo. If anyone promises that they can do it for much less, be sure you check them out really thoroughly before you give them any money. Ask to listen to other demos they've produced. Go on line and see if anyone's heard of them or worked with them before. Once again, the Internet is your greatest resource, and the community you find there can be your family.

Remember, the more planning, research, and rehearsal you do before you start, the more money you'll save in the end. You don't want to show up in the studio to record and still be tweaking your scripts. The clock will be ticking the whole time, and you'll be paying for it.

By investing in a professional, high quality demo, you're showing the people who will be listening to it that you're serious about voice acting. You'll also be showing *yourself* that you're serious, and that knowledge is going to be worth at least as much as convincing the pros who do the hiring. By the same token, putting out a shoddy demo may make those listening to it think that you're neither serious nor professional. And rarely, if ever, does someone like that get hired.

Your demo is your calling card, your vanguard, your invitation to the world to come to your party. Since your demo says *this is me*, make sure it truly represents how professional, how talented, how unique and cool you truly are.

GET TO THE POINT

When I first made up my demo reel and started to send it out, I had huge expectations for it. I had put a lot of money, time, and energy into its creation and I was terribly proud of it. I knew that it had been put together professionally and really showed off my voice. It was a *two and a half minute* celebration of what I could do! I mailed it out across town to various agents and sat back, waiting for the phone to ring.

And I waited.

And waited.

Nothing. Not a peep. I made a few follow-up calls to some of my top-choice agencies in the hopes that they were just slow getting in touch, but their response was, "Oh, we'll call if we're interested," or "It sounded good, but we already have several of your type." Not responses I wanted to hear.

I was bummed. And had to come up with a solution fast. Then I remembered overhearing someone once say, "Just get to the point already." I knew what I had to do.

Knowing that I was too close emotionally to the product, I found an engineer who wouldn't have any previous knowledge of my reel, and asked him to order and re-cut the clips into a *one* minute reel. His ear honed in on the short catchy spots, and he reorganized and trimmed my material to get the listener engaged right away.

I sent this abridged version out, and within a week I had found my voice-over agent! Sometimes just giving folks what they need/want to hear gets them hooked and curious far faster than overloading them with tons of variety.

TARA PLATT, ACTRESS

SHORT AND SWEET

A parting note on demos: keep 'em short. In this bit-per-second world we live in, the folks listening to your demo will get all the info they need within a few seconds, so a good length per spot may be only six to eight or ten seconds, tops. You can *record* a longer spot or sample if you'd like, but then pull only the *very best part* of that to showcase on your reel. The length of a narration sample will be longer (perhaps a twenty second clip), but when in doubt, cut it down.

The times, they are a-changin'. It used to be that a person's demo might be much longer, but short is the new black. Try, if possible, to get the length of your entire demo down to around one minute (that's sixty seconds, in case you're counting) per category: commercial, animation, etc. If you create a demo that has multiple tracks on it (a commercial track, an animation track, a narration track) you may of course have a minute per track.

We recommend that you visit our Web sites (TaraPlatt.com and YuriLowenthal.com) and listen to our commercial demo reels so that you can hear an example of a professionally produced demo filled with a variety of tracks (yes, we wrote all those commercials ourselves, and yes, Yuri's commercial demo is much longer than a minute). We also recommend stopping by VideoVoiceBank.net to listen to other actors' demos.

One thing you may notice when you listen to our demos is that we put things that make us happy in them. You can let that be your guide, too. Let your personality shine, use your imagination, and have fun building this little ark that you're going to send out into the world.

CHAPTER 11
AGENTS/MANAGERS & PERSONAL MARKETING

"Success doesn't come to you... you go to it."

MARVA COLLINS, U.S. EDUCATOR

"WHO'S IN MY CORNER?"

This acting stuff is hard work. You're going to want to start building a team of people who will help you so that you don't have to go it alone. First, let's talk about these mysterious agents and managers, aka *your representation*. You're eventually going to want someone like this working for you for a couple of reasons:

1. You don't have time to hustle and negotiate 24/7; you want someone else to be carrying some of that weight.

2. These people have access to job information that you most likely will *not* have access to.

Having a rep who knows about jobs you don't know about, and hustles for you to get them, should be worth the 10-15% he or she is going to take off the top. In the end, a small price to pay if they keep you working.

"Do I Need Representation?"

No. You don't necessarily need representation – certainly not when you're just starting out. The truth is, you can do much of the legwork on your own, and book plenty of work without a go-between. And having an agent or a manager doesn't mean that you won't still have to do your own hustling on top of that. But if you really want to be making a living at voice work, you're eventually going to need representation of some sort.

So many jobs put out casting calls only to agencies. If you want a crack at those jobs, you'll need an agent. Of course, not all jobs come through agents. Many you will end up auditioning for because of your personal relationship with a director or a studio, or even from trolling craigslist.org. But you want to make yourself as available as you can to every opportunity, and being represented by a competent agent or manager can greatly increase those opportunities.

Some actors feel more professional or *safer* if they are represented by an agency, and make finding an agent a priority. Other actors try to get work on their own first and look for representation when the time seems right – or better yet, hope that representation finds *them* because of the work they've done. This is a personal decision and is different for every actor. No matter how you cut it, though, if you want to succeed, you will have to work at getting jobs on your own.

We've heard it said, "An agent gets only 10%, so expect them to do only 10% of the work." Just because you find representation with an agency does not mean that you should kick back, relax, and wait for them to bring you all of your work. Agents can be extremely helpful, but you're still the CEO of You, Inc. An agent or manager is part of your work staff.

We haven't really explained how agents and managers differ. Managers are more a part of the on-camera acting world than the voice-over world: you hardly hear of voice-over managers. But, so that you understand the difference, here's the scoop.

Compared to an agent, a manager is less responsible for finding you individual jobs, and more responsible for managing your overall career, making sure you pick projects that take you in the right direction to build a successful livelihood. For this special attention, they usually require a 15% cut of any work you do.

An agent's job, on the other hand, is a little more specific: to find you work, plain and simple. This is not to say that agents don't care about your overall success, but their main concern (for which they generally require a 10% cut) is finding you jobs. They will try to find auditions that are best suited to your abilities, but they are less concerned with creating a brand for you or with other aspects of your career.

A manager technically can't legally negotiate contracts, while the agent can, but those lines can get blurry. Some actors have both an agent *and* a manager. You might not need that until you're a big shot, but some actors like to have as many people working for them as possible, and who can blame them? Sure, you'll be paying a manager's and an agent's cut, but wouldn't you rather pay 25% of *some*thing, than 0% of *no*thing? Most importantly, as much as it seems like the manager and agent have power over you, you must remember at all times that you're not working for them: *they're working for you.*

"WHERE DO I FIND THEM?"

Where will you find this elusive agent to represent you? Well, much like the VO auditions, the VO representatives tend to be located in the cities where the most work is going on. That means you could have an agent in L.A., New York, and/or Chicago, for example. You can find lists of accredited agencies through the union (SAG, AFTRA ...) Web sites, publications like *Ross Reports* or the *Voice Over Resource Guide*. (More information on these publications can be found in the *Resources* section at the end of this book.)

Some of the larger voice-over agencies may have offices in several cities, say, L.A. and New York, or maybe even London. However, just because an agent is bi-coastal or multi-continental doesn't mean you are automatically represented in all of those cities if you're repped in one. Be sure you ask about things like that before signing your contract with an agency.

Here's something for you to remember: *never pay someone to represent you.* If a potential agent or manager asks for any kind of money up front, whether it's for *operating expenses* or *postage* or whatever, just politely walk away because *they are not legit.* If they say that to sign with them you are required to take classes with a specific teacher or record your demo with a specific person, just politely walk away because *they are not legit.*

Sure, legitimate reps may say it would be a *good idea* for you to take a class, and often they will have a list of people they know to be good. But anyone who insists that you study or work with *their guy* might be getting a kickback from these people. Reps should make money only when you make money.

We repeat: *never pay someone to represent you.* It may seem tempting, but we have never once heard of anything good coming of it. And we've heard a lot of horror stories.

From the Agent's Desk

My most successful clients are the ones who make strong choices for auditions and stick with them. They don't over-think the audition and wonder how many different ways they could've done it. They visualize what the end product will be and then do their best to provide that. After the audition, they walk away and don't think about it again. It's this particular mind-set of being confident in one's performance and not worrying about the outcome that is the best attitude for success in this business.

BRADFORD BRICKEN, AGENT

SELF-PROMOTION 101

Self-promotion can be hard for some people. It takes work. And how many times did your grandma say, "People don't want to hear you talk about yourself!" We're taught that *tooting our own horn* is prideful and unattractive. But in this business, you have to find as many ways as possible to let people know how great you are and why they should be hiring you. And as we said before, promoting you is not part of your agent's job. What if you don't even have an agent? What can you do on your own? Well, a lot, actually.

We'll talk about some of the things you can do to promote yourself, but there are plenty more ideas beyond what we'll go into. The more creative you get, the more effective your promotion will be. So put your fun-hat on and get cranking on some ideas.

Once you've determined what your sound is and decided where you think you might fit best in the VO market, you're done with the hard part. Use this info to promote yourself and move in the direction you want.

MIC SAYS: Don't worry if you don't have an agent yet: you'll always be your own best promoter. So start selling yourself now.

WHAT TO DO WITH YOUR DEMO

So what do you do with your masterpiece? The demo you spent all that love, time, energy, and dough on? You get it out there and get it working for you. It's time to try to get a return on your investment.

Do a mailing to your target agents or managers, and don't stop there. Do a little research, and target production studios, ad agencies, producers, casting agents, and directors who work on the kind of projects that you'd like to be working on. Once again, feel free to check out the *Resources* section of this book to get more direction about where you can start your search.

Post your reel on line; it's easy these days. Make it accessible on Facebook, MySpace, LinkedIn, Twitter, and any other online social networking site, so that if someone wants to hear it, they can find it easily. Build your own Web site and host your demo there. The more online places your demo is featured and associated with your name, the easier it is for somebody to find it by using a search engine like Google.

Use whatever method you can think of to get your demo into the hands of the people who could hire you (or at least into the hands of someone who can introduce you to some of those people). There is no right or wrong way to do this, but there *is* a fine line between *catchy* and *gimmicky* – much like the line between *aggressively pursuing* and *stalking*. So do be respectful about putting yourself in people's faces.

We've found that the difference between catchy and gimmicky can be crystallized in this comparison: a personalized card with a funny note included with your demo is fine; a glitter-filled envelope that explodes all over an agent's desk when he or she opens it will get you remembered, but for all the wrong reasons ...

A short note on packaging: except for those times when you simply e-mail your demo as an MP3, you'll need some sort of packaging for it. You'll want it to look nice and professional. Feel free to use your creativity in putting your package together, but one word of warning: while it may *seem* to be a good idea to put a *picture* of you somewhere on that CD case, listen when we say that there are better options. Putting your face on your demo automatically typecasts you in the eyes of the person looking at it. As a voice actor you want a potential employer to think that you can be anything and anyone.

If agents have a specific image of you in their heads, it'll be harder for them to consider you as anything other than what you look like. We've been telling you how important it is to use your imagination, right? Well, let the agents use their imaginations this time.

WEB SITE

Nowadays a Web presence is practically essential for anyone trying to market themselves in this business. It serves as your calling card and news feed, letting people know what you're up to. As we've mentioned, the Web provides a way for new people to find you, and it's a fantastic place to post your demo reel for quick and easy access by potential employers.

Once you have a Web site set up, you can make a business card that includes your Web address (preferably an address that's your name, like *ArchibaldTuttle.com* or *TaraPlatt.com*, although sometimes, if that's not an option, you'll have to get creative: *ArchibaldTuttleVO.com* or *YuriLowenthalIsAVoiceActor.com*). Then, whenever you meet people in the VO business, you can give them your card: suddenly all your info is at their fingertips.

Even the most basic Web site should include your name, general contact info (phone number, e-mail, etc.) and/or your representation contact info. In addition it might also include a list of credits and/or upcoming work, and maybe a clip or a demo reel of your voice.

Many actors choose not to have images of themselves on their Web sites if the site is for voice-over only, as one of the great things about voice-over is that it isn't looks-based (remember our note about packaging). Instead of displaying your photo, you can put up images that showcase either the work you've done or the qualities or essence your voice evokes.

Your Web site may feature several different things ranging from your professional acting experience to your personal life. If so, make sure that it's as easy to navigate to your VO info as possible, so that potential employers don't get caught up in photos of your latest class reunion when all they're trying to do is listen to your VO demo. If possible, you might want to have a separate site for your personal stuff so that professionals visiting your VO site don't see anything that might adversely affect their judgment of you: those photos may be funny to you and your friends, but a casting director might not get the joke.

You don't have to spend a lot of money, nor do you need to know html programming to set up a decent, effective Web site that you'll be able to update yourself. Shop around, ask around, and find a Web hosting company that works for you. Check out other actors' sites, and if you like what you see, shoot some of them an e-mail and ask who's hosting their Web sites and who did the design (sometimes you'll find that information at the bottom of the Web page). There are even companies that let you design your own *free* Web page, and that can help when you're trying to get started on the cheap. In any case, creating a page is something you can do on your own. And a Web site is a resource that could prove very important. So full steam ahead!

POSTCARDS AND BUSINESS CARDS

In addition to having an online presence, having something a little more tangible as either an introduction or a follow-up can often be useful as well. Consider it the old-school approach.

A business card is good to have when you're meeting someone in person. Having something physical like that can be even more effective sometimes than, say, an e-mail. When the people you give your card to get home, they empty their pockets and the card sits on their desks, or counters, or bedside tables, in full view – and hopefully keeps you fresh in their minds long enough for you to get lodged there.

In addition to listing your basic contact info (name, phone number, e-mail address, Web site) on your business card, you might even summarize your voice signature with a couple of key words that best describe your vocal quality. A card like that will help people identify you easily. At least at first you'll want people to associate you with a specific characteristic, so that when they're looking for, say, *spunky*, they think of you. Put that characteristic on your card, keep some cards in your wallet; and when you meet someone, you'll have just the thing to help them remember you. You might even slip a business card into a letter or demo mailing.

Your postcard should have the same info that's on your business card, and it'll give you a little more room to be creative. For example, if you've done any work recently, you can write, "Hey, just did this job!" or "Check me out in this show/game/commercial!"

A postcard can be used as a follow-up to a demo mailing or after a meeting. You might even send your postcard as an introduction before you send your demo. The agent might get the card, go to your Web site (the Web address *is* on your postcard, right?), listen to your demo on line, and you won't have to send that agent your reel at all. (Don't assume that'll happen. Agents and casting directors are busy people. They don't always have time to type in a Web address found on a postcard; but a physical CD is easy for them to pop into their computer.)

Business cards and postcards make it easy for you to keep in touch. And maybe even more important, they make it easy for people to keep in touch with you.

The Mailing: Ships out to Sea

Dallas Travers, an acting-career coach and good friend of ours, fondly calls mailings, "sending your ships out to sea," which we think is a wonderful analogy. You have to be prepared for some of those ships to get lost at sea, or for the cargo not to be what the port needed at that time. But some of those ships you send off just may find their way through treacherous waters and dock at the perfect spot, making your sailing – ahem, *mailing* – pay off.

Many of your postcards or demos may not make it to the agent's or CD's office; but remember, sometimes it only takes one. You put all that work into your demo, so you might as well send it out there: that's what it's for. Thankfully, envelopes, postcards, and demos are cheaper than ships ...

NETWORK, NETWORK, NETWORK

Many people snidely call this *schmooooozing*, but the truth is, meeting people and developing relationships is how things get done in the entertainment business. Practicing good solid networking skills can help you move forward quickly and consciously toward the next level of your career.

Networking facilitates your being in the right place at the right time. This is part of the preparation + opportunity (*right place at the right time*) = success equation. Prepare yourself, and then put yourself in situations where you can mingle and meet people. Sometimes you can target the people you want to work with. But honestly, you never know where a job or an important friendship is going to come from. So don't limit your interactions.

How do you go about schmoozing? Well, first off, let's stop calling it that. Let's opt for *networking*. The word schmoozing has always carried a negative connotation to us because it implies that you're forcing yourself onto other people for the sole purpose of getting something from them; and that's just kind of slimy. That's probably why a lot of actors have trouble networking – because when it's called schmoozing, they feel like they're doing something gross. The less pressure you put on meeting people, the easier it's going to be, and the better it'll probably work out.

Where do you go to network? There are a variety of places to go and ways to make connections happen. Search for networking events and social gatherings specifically geared toward voice-over and voice acting or to entertainment in general. These events are often listed in entertainment trade papers and on Web sites, and will certainly be more plentiful in big cities like New York and Los Angeles.

Don't look just for parties (which are sometimes hard to get into). Find out where the people that you would like to work with hang out, and go there. Get yourself in the same circles they're in and see what happens. You don't have to be in a big city to make this work. You can go out with friends who are also working in the business, and meet the people they know. If you don't know anyone else who's interested in voice acting or in what you want to be doing, then *find them*.

Put an ad in a local paper or post it on an online site, somewhere like craigslist or Facebook. Set up a gathering for people interested in the same things you're interested in. Build a support group, if you will. Things happen much faster (and it's usually more fun) if you've got a whole group working at it. Who knows, the group you assemble might end up producing a cartoon together.

If you network well, and don't put pressure on a specific outcome, it won't be perceived as *schmoozy*. Still it's not always the easiest thing for some people to do. Networking might not come naturally for you, so pay attention to people who are good at it and learn from them. In the end, being yourself is the best thing you can do when you meet and socialize with people professionally. You don't need to try to act cool so they'll like you. Remember you have as much to offer them as they have to offer you.

Networking should never be about what you can *get* from others. Treat them as you would your friends, and be friendly and personable. You just may be someone they will want to befriend and (who knows?) maybe work with one day.

And don't forget your cards! A networking event is a perfect opportunity to get your business cards into people's hands. Think of this as sowing seeds.

You may have to plant a few seeds before anything starts growing. You never know which seed will grow and bear fruit, so sprinkle those seeds liberally. The more seeds – um, *business cards* – you hand out, the better your chances are. And if other people give you their cards, be sure to follow up and let them know that you enjoyed meeting them. Then file the cards away somewhere that you'll be able to find them again, just in case you want to get in touch. You can use your new postcards to follow up with those new contacts you made while networking.

SWAG

Ah, swag. The sometimes unique-and-catchy, sometimes obnoxious-and-kitschy gift that you can use to promote yourself. We'll touch on this only briefly because we've never employed this method ourselves. We do, however, know actors who have tried it, and we still remember their swag; so it must work for some people.

Often, actors will use swag in an attempt to brand themselves and become more memorable or easily recognizable. For example, an actress we know has a name that bears a resemblance to that of a popular candy bar, so she had candy bar labels (and matching business cards) printed up with her name in a similar font and gave out chocolates as a fun, silly gift. A pair of married voice actors we know also had candy bar labels made up showing them as superheroes (why didn't we think of that?). If we've learned anything here, it's that people love chocolate; and if you can get them to tie you to something they already love, well then, you're halfway there.

Other folks have created magnets, mugs, self-modeled bobblehead dolls, or even brewed their own beers to give to people they work with and *want* to work with. Studios and agencies can quickly become museums of interesting (and sometimes odd) swag created by actors. It can be a great way to stand out, but you don't want to become known just as "that actor who gives out flashlights."*

Before sending out swag, first make sure that anything you choose to give is relatively related to what you want to say about yourself. Second, be sure that you can back up your swag with real talent because that's ultimately what you want to be remembered for.

*Unless your last name is Flashlight, in which case we sincerely apologize.

YOUR CONTACT INFO

If you're on the lam or in a witness protection program, you want to be as difficult to find as possible. Not so in this business. Just the opposite, as a matter of fact. And to help people find you as easily as possible (until you get famous, and then you can go back to making yourself difficult to find), do your best to keep your contact details constant and available. By that we mean make sure your contact information is out there and easy to find when someone's looking for you; and if possible, don't go changing it every six months or even every year.

Sometimes it takes a while for those seeds you spread to grow into trees you can swing from (okay, maybe we've taken this analogy too far). If someone you've handed your business card to tries to call you, and all they hear is, "You have reached a number that has been disconnected or is no longer in service ...," odds are they aren't going to keep looking for you. It takes too much effort, too much time, and this is a fast-moving business. They've probably got a stack of similar business cards and they're already on to the next one.

Changing your contact info will end up costing you more than just work. It will be very expensive for you to have to change the information on your business cards, postcards, demos, and anything else you may have already printed with your now out-dated info on it.

If you absolutely *must* change your contact info, make sure you update it on your Web site, and even send out an e-mail blast letting everyone know that you've changed it. You never know when that call's going to come. Make sure it gets through.

Union/Nonunion

Whether or not to join a union is a question that will come up eventually, and everybody's got a strong opinion on it. So rather than try to tell you how to play your cards, we'll just go over some basic information.

In the U.S., many jobs in professional voice-over are regulated by either the Screen Actors Guild (*SAG*) or the American Federation of Television and Radio Artists (*AFTRA*). To work on a SAG job, you must be a member of SAG; and to work on an AFTRA job, you must be a member of AFTRA. To get more details on these unions and their regulations, please visit their respective Web sites (*www.SAG.org* and *www.AFTRA.com*).

In other countries the jurisdiction may fall to unions such as the Alliance of Canadian Cinema Television and Radio Artists (ACTRA), and the British Academy of Film and Television Arts (BAFTA). Check to see what union might apply in your country.

Some employers may choose to go *non*union, meaning that only people *not* belonging to a union may apply. If you are just starting out in the U.S., odds are you will belong to neither union and your only option will be to work nonunion jobs. There's nothing wrong with this, despite the fact that union work will seem like the Holy Grail to you because of the benefits and the often higher pay scale.

Don't obsess over joining the union. That time will come when it's right. If you force your way there before you're ready, you may find yourself in a different pinch: now you're limited to union work only, but you have no agent, haven't built a name for yourself, nor have you amassed many contacts. So how are you going to get this union work? You're better off working the jobs you can until the opportunity to join a union presents itself naturally. The nonunion work is out there. And some of it pays as well as union work.

Once again, if you *are* in the union, you cannot work on nonunion jobs that would be covered by that union.

All union jobs (jobs under that union's jurisdiction) are paid the same basic scale rate for the same type of job, so you will always be assured that Job X = $Y. No one else will be getting paid a different amount for doing the same type of job. A common exception, of course, is a well-known or celebrity talent who may be able to negotiate a higher rate. The union is also responsible for making sure working conditions are safe and that the needs of its membership are taken care of.

Similarly, if you are *nonunion*, you cannot work on union jobs and usually can't even *audition* for union jobs. There are, however, exceptions to this rule. For example, if you are nonunion, but have a specific skill or talent that is hard to find, an employer may be willing to pay a fee and *buy* your way into the union if they exhaust their union options without finding someone suitable for the job.

Say producers of a video game are looking for an actor who speaks fluent Tupi from South America – but specifically Guarani dialect, not Nheengatu. They hold auditions for union actors who speak Guarani, and don't find any. But the video game *requires* it. Now they've got to look further afield, and if you're a nonunion actor who speaks Guarani, you may be in luck. This may be your golden ticket. Book this union job and you can start the process of becoming a union member.

And that's another reason to be a well-rounded actor with many interests and skills. Not only will it make you more interesting as a person (and hence, actor), but your odd hobby might pay off in ways you could never imagine.

A common misconception about nonunion jobs is that they pay less than union jobs. This is often the case, but not always. They will sometimes pay more than union jobs since they aren't regulated; but a nonunion job without regulations might mean you are working longer hours or under conditions that aren't up to the standard of union requirements. Many studios will have both types of work depending on the producers and the clients they work with.

We can't say that there is a cap to the limit of success you can attain by staying nonunion, but we have noticed that most of the working actors we know have had to join the union at some point in order to keep their careers moving along. The choicest jobs are most often the union ones. Don't let this be a hindrance. Let it be a goal. One that you will reach when the time is right.

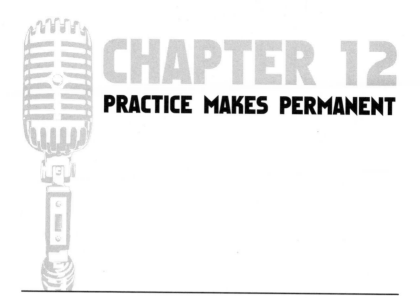

CHAPTER 12
PRACTICE MAKES PERMANENT

"Desire is the key to motivation, but it's the determination and commitment to an unrelenting pursuit of your goal – a commitment to excellence – that will enable you to attain the success you seek."

MARIO ANDRETTI, ITALIAN-AMERICAN
CHAMPION AUTO RACER

Time to take the stuff we've talked about and practice on some real live scripts, since the best way to be comfortable and confident when you get in the booth is to have practiced beforehand. But before we throw you into the fire, let's give you a little lesson on hieroglyphics. Okay, well, maybe not hieroglyphics *exactly*, but the first time you see certain kinds of script notations it might feel like you're dealing with a new language. These cryptic markings on your script are there to make things easier on you. Let's take a look at them now so you're ready to translate them when the time comes.

SCRIPT NOTATIONS

Script notations are used to give you, the actor, a heads-up about such things as where there are pauses in a line of dialogue and how long the pauses are. There are some notations to let you know if your character has an intake of breath or some sort of reaction, and still others to indicate what the character's mouth looks like on screen so you can best match the lip flap.

The notations themselves can differ slightly from original animation to dub work, from video game to commercial, from writer to writer, and even studio to studio. We're going to introduce you to some that we see most frequently, especially working in ADR/dubbing. Let this list be a general guide, but as always, never hesitate to ask the director what a notation means if you're unfamiliar with it.

TIME CODE

In the corner at the top or bottom of the screen might be a black box with numbers in it showing the *time code*. The time code indicates how far the program/movie has progressed, and enables everyone to stay on the same page. The numbers break down into *Hour:Minute:Second:Frame* so that if, for example, you have a line for which the time code is *01:02:03:04*, that means the line would begin at one hour, two minutes, three seconds, and four frames into the movie/program. Hours, minutes, and seconds, you're probably pretty familiar with; but *frames*? Allow us to explain.

When dealing with a recorded moving image (film/video/ animation), the illusion of movement is essentially created by flashing still images in rapid succession (hence the term *moving pictures*). This process fools the human eye – in much the same way an old-fashioned flip book did. Only these days, we're talking much more high tech, with the individual images, or *frames*, generally going by at a rate of twenty-four or thirty per second. Because these frames go by so fast, you need not concern yourself too much with the frame number in the time code. That number will be much more important to the engineer, who may have to make very specific adjustments to lines that you'll record.

The engineer will always cue you up to the correct time code so that The Three Beeps bring you in at the exact moment you need to speak. Sometimes a script will show both an *in* and an *out* code so that you know when to begin speaking and also when to be done. The notation *01:03:12:19 – 01:03:25:20* indicates that the line begins at one hour, three minutes, twelve seconds and nineteen frames, and ends at one hour, three minutes, twenty-five seconds and twenty frames, giving you about thirteen seconds to speak.

LINE OR LOOP NUMBERS

A *loop number* or *line number* is just another number (usually found to the left of each line in the script) that makes it easier for the director/engineer/actor to refer to a specific line. Lines are numbered in consecutive order. Sometimes, when a line has been added after the original script was written, the new line number might be followed by a letter to avoid confusion (e.g. 1, 2, 3, *3A*, *3B*, 4, 5 …).

MOUTH MOVEMENT

When recording *to picture* (recording dialogue to what has already been animated or filmed), you might encounter notations specifically dealing with a character's mouth movement, or lip flap. Below we list some of the most common notations.

MNS is short for *mouth not seen*, and indicates that the character's *mouth* is not visible, even though he/she/it might be on screen at the time. Perhaps his or her face is turned away from the camera, or there's something blocking it from view – like a fan or a giant sword for example. The *MNS* loop can be a boon to actors because you won't need to pay attention to mouth flap; you need be concerned only with timing. Similar to this notation is *MBS*, or *mouth barely seen*. This refers to when the character's mouth is so far away you can barely see it move, even if it is flapping.

Similar to *MNS* are the straightforward notations *OFF* and *ON* which mean exactly what each word indicates: the line is spoken either *off*screen or *on*-screen. (The notation *OS* is also used for *offscreen*.) Sometimes both of these notations are used in the same loop. An example: a character wanders offscreen and then back on again, or an on-screen character turns away from the camera for a portion of the line.

Sometimes an even shorter shorthand is used to indicate an *off* line: underlining. Underlining comes in handy particularly in the above-mentioned case, where some of the line is *on* and some of it is *off*. An example of an *on-off-on* line might look like this on the script:

"You know <u>you'll never be able to get away with</u> that, Toshi, you're gonna get caught."

This gives you a heads-up that you'll have to pay particular attention to the mouth flaps at the beginning and at the end, but that several mouth flaps in the middle, you won't see at all. This notation can become confusing if a writer is also using underlining to indicate to the actor that a certain word should be stressed, but this is only rarely a problem.

CM indicates a *closed mouth*. "How would that apply to someone speaking?" you ask. Well, remember, not all lines involve speaking. Many of them involve things like laughing, grunting, or humming. So if you see a notation that says, *CM grunt* or *CM chuckle*, you know that the mouth won't be flapping, and that you should grunt or chuckle with your mouth closed. Similarly, you might see *OM*, *open mouth*, to denote the opposite.

CT is similar to closed mouth, but means *closed/clenched teeth*. Pull your lips back like you're growling or snarling: that's pretty much what CT is going to look like. Some people can speak through clenched teeth. Some can laugh. Some can only growl. Give it a shot; see what you can do with your teeth clenched.

Other notations you'll come across in your script might include *reax* – shorthand for *reaction* (e.g. *fight reax*, *fear reax*), *sigh*, *thought filter* (which denotes that the mouth won't be flapping even though there's dialogue because the dialogue is going on inside the character's head), or *inhale/exhale*.

HITCHES

Standard punctuation can't always be trusted to ensure that a phrase times out (synchronizes) with action that's happening on the screen. To help you match specific timing, notations called *hitches* are included in the script. Hitches warn you of breaks in the line (pauses within a line of dialogue). You'll have to pay attention to these breaks/pauses when you're trying to match specific timing. Some of these notations might appear as one of the following marks: - ' ^ / ... and they all indicate varying lengths of pauses. Different writers will sometimes notate hitches differently, so you'll have to stay on your toes.

When considering the length of a pause, the idea of a *beat* (about a second) is a pretty good starting point. Often, if a director just wants a *slight* hitch, he or she actually wants less than a second. A shorter hitch is usually indicated by one of these marks ^ *or* ' while either / *or* ... may be used for longer pauses.

SOMETIMES IT ALL JUST WORKS ANYWAY

We dubbed the original *Voltron* series without seeing it. In those days, anime was new and there were no set systems for doing it. So the writer would watch the show and use the time code to time each line by frames, then convert it to seconds. In the script, next to each line of dialogue, he would place a number such as 5.46 or 1.23 indicating seconds, tenths and hundredths of seconds.

When the actors went in to record, they would *not* see a video of the show. There were no monitors at all. Instead, the director, Franklin Cofod, would have a stopwatch, and each time the actor said his line, Franklin would time it and check the stopwatch. If it matched the number on the script, he'd move on. If it didn't match, he'd redo the line until it matched. Pauses were not indicated, so the actors would talk right thru pauses. As new characters came in or out of the series, there were no visuals or audio for the actors to go on, so they had to guess at what the character would sound like. Often they'd use a little weaselly voice for a big burly character or a childish voice for an old man.

The result of all this should have been disastrous. Instead *Voltron* was a mega-hit show – once again proving Henslowe's theory in *Shakespeare in Love*, "Strangely enough, it all turns out well ... It's a mystery."

MARC HANDLER, DIRECTOR

PRACTICE SCRIPT AND COPY SECTION

You will want to get your hands on as much copy and as many scripts as you can to familiarize yourself with the work you'll be doing. Although each project is unique and each session will have its own specialized copy, reading through a variety of scripts before you start working will get your brain going as well as your mouth, and you will find that you'll be more comfortable when you actually need to read a script for work.

As you know by now, *copy* is the material you will be working on in an audition or recording session. Below you will find some examples of various types of copy with which to put your VO skills to the test. You might want to use a similar variety for the clips on your demo reel.

You should notice that each example below has a different feel to it. The feel of a scene or phrase can indicate the types of vocal qualities you might want to employ when reading it.

MIC SAYS: Specs are a good starting point, but ad execs don't always know what they want; so don't be afraid to bring your own magic to the material.

COMMERCIAL COPY

Following is a series of different types of commercial spots you might come across, from hard sell to soft sell. The most important thing to remember is that with all commercial copy, personalizing the identity of the individual you're giving the information to can make the copy come to life. In our examples, we give you a spec to use as a jumping off point; but after you've tried it our way, feel free to bring your own ideas to the copy to give yourself more of a workout.

Hamburking Burgers

Spec: Cool, laid back, talking to your buddy

The cheapest place to get a burger is also the healthiest place to get a burger. At Hamburking Burgers. We only sell burgers. And for just 99 cents. All natural, all fresh, all fast. A Burger for a buck. Yeah!

Alive Insurance

Spec: Honest, folksy, wise

Your family is more important than anything, and luckily, now you have someone who thinks you're just as important as they are. At Alive Insurance, it's our goal to make sure you and your entire family are protected through life's many adventures. Call your Alive Insurance Representative today at 800-555-1234 to find out how you can make the most of tomorrow – today.

HipKool Back-to-School Clothes

Spec: High energy, fast-paced, hip and fun, but not cartoony

Right now at HipKool all the coolest clothes are 30-50% off. That's right, just 30-50% off. And if you come in this Saturday you'll find clothes for him at an additional 10% off. Girls get an additional 20% off all accessories and jewelry. So come on down and get all the best back-to-school gear this weekend just in time to show off your new jeans. And with all his-and-her denim for less than 30 bucks, there'll be plenty to show off. The HipKool Back-to-School shop-off, now thru August 30th, and with additional 10-20% discounts this Saturday. Get back-to-school savings at HipKool.

Awesome Action Toys

Spec: High energy, aggro, X-games-type read, but not shouting

You can jump 'em! You can rock 'em! You can roll 'em! Cool Wheel Carz! For the lightning-fast action of a real race, use them on dirt, water, or grass! See if you can win the race! Cars and racetrack sold separately. Cool Wheel Carz a division of Awesome Action Toys.

Diabetes PSA

Spec: Personal, confessional, genuine

I still remember the smell of smoke on a crisp, cool, autumn evening, the sounds of laughter coming from the house, my sister and me eating fudge and marshmallows 'til our tummies hurt. I lost my sister to her fight against diabetes almost 2 years ago, and it could have been prevented. With almost 8% of the U.S. population currently diagnosed with diabetes, there's no time like the present to deal with this growing disease. Now more than ever, we need your support to fund vital diabetes research and save the future of our children.

Equator Flyy Travel Site

Spec: Wry, simple, not too charactery

Let Equator Flyy take you around the world for less than $2000. With round-trip fares from tons of major U.S. cities to destinations in Mexico, Australia, and Europe, getting away has never been so easy. Just visit us at EquatorFlyyTravel.com and click on "Around the World" to see our latest deals and destinations.

Bank 'R Us Tag

Spec: Fast-paced, intelligent, factual

Bank 'R Us Banking is a Member FDIC, Equal Opportunity Lender. Products and services are offered by Bank 'R Us Banking and its affiliates. Programs, fees, rates, and features are subject to change without notice.

ANIMATION SCRIPTS

Remember when we told you there are original animation (pre-lay) jobs and dubbed animation jobs, and that there are differences between recording them? Well, now's our chance to show you how the *copy* for each of these jobs differs as well. The content may be similar, but the scripts look very different, and the way you read them won't always be the same.

Original

We've dusted off an old script from an animated show called *Yuratari the Goat* – okay, so we just made it up. But humor us and just imagine for a moment that it's an excerpt from a pre-lay animation script.

<u>EXT. DEEP DARK WOODS NEAR THE FORTRESS OF EVIL – DUSK</u>

Sam and Yuratari the Goat look at the fortress, black smoke rising from behind its walls.

245   SAM

    We're not gonna be able to make it!

246   YURATARI

    Baaaah! We can do it. You go down that side
    and I'll come at them from the front.

247   SAM

    Aren't you worried they'll see you?

248   YURATARI

    I'm more worried about what might happen
    if we don't get the Crystal of Light back soon
    – Baaaaaah.

Sam reluctantly turns and starts to run to the gorge.

249   SAM

                (turning back)

    Be careful you crazy goat. I don't wanna
    have to tell Princess Mona you didn't make it
    back!

                        FADE TO BLACK

Dubbed animation

We can't very well include *actual* copy from a series we're working on, so let's pretend we just licensed a new Japanese animated show that's being dubbed into English. Below is some of this exciting copy from *Best Dub Show Happy Time, Go!* Enjoy...

Loop Number	Time Code	Character	Line	Notes
4.	01:12:27:21 01:12:29:24	Kira	Stop right there!	*Very frightened*
5.	01:12:30:07 01:12:34:09	Suki	What? ^ No, it can't be.	
6.	01:12:35:18 01:12:38:10	Suki	Is it ... ^ (OM SURPRISE REAX)	*mouth moves a lot on reax*
7.	01:12:39:05 01:12:43:07	Kira	Why do you look at me like that?	
8.	01:12:45:09 01:12:49:18	Kira	(thought filter) What a strange girl this is.	
9.	01:12:50:03 01:12:53:05	Suki	It's you. / The Chicken ^ of Destiny.	
10.	01:12:55:15 01:12:57:10	Kira	(CT DISGUST REAX) How dare you!	*dialogue a little fast*
11.	01:12:59:01 01:13:02:20	Suki	I am dishonored!	

VIDEO GAME SCRIPT

Each video game session is different, but many of the scripts we've worked with recently actually have each character's lines separated from the rest of the script to make it easier to record them all at a run. That said, for the video game dialogue below, let's say you've been asked to do an ABC (series) take of each of the efforts as small, medium, and large.

To explore a variety of sounds, imagine different types of

movements your character might be making. Are you blocking a hit with your arm or your leg? Do you take the hit to your gut, your chest, or your head? This distinction will affect the reaction sound you create and help differentiate your efforts. Variety will get you rehired.

When you come across lines in the script that describe only the *type* of effort or sound they want you to make (e.g. *attack, throwing effort, fall, jump, death*), you should not only remember to really go for it, but imagine a variety of different vocalizations for each effort. Consider different consonant and vowel combinations. Getting hit in the stomach could sound like *ooof!* but it could also be *aargh!* or *kugh!* Perhaps an attack might sound like *hyyyah!* or *raah!chuh!*

Line #	Character	Dialogue	
15	MELCHIOR	Never! We will take this ship...	
16	MELCHIOR	(Shoving effort)	3x
17	MELCHIOR	(Attack)	3x
18	MELCHIOR	Yield, or perish!	
19	MELCHIOR	(Take damage)	3x
20	MELCHIOR	See you on the other side of hell!	
21	MELCHIOR	(War cry)	3x
22	MELCHIOR	I never... thought... I'd hear you say--	
23	MELCHIOR	(Death)	3x

PROMO/TRAILER COPY

Similar to commercial copy, but specifically promoting a particular network or TV show, the promos below give you just a taste of this type of copy.

The YT Network

Spec: Real, Hip, Girl/Guy-next-door, ex. Jennifer Garner, Justin Long

WhyTea? Just because. Check it out. Only on YT.

Check it. The funny. Why? Tea. Only on YT.

Coming up next, on YT. Check it.

The Toppies Award Show

Ladies and Gentlemen, please take your seats, sit back, and enjoy the most riveting, most exhilarating, most action-packed awards show this season. The Toppies, the top awards given to the best, the brightest, and the most promising actors, writers, directors, and engineers in the field of voice-over. First up for Best Female Performance in an animated series ...

Tumbling After *Trailer*

In a world where darkness meets light, one man is forced to choose between the two. A dark secret will threaten to tear these two lovers apart. Will Jack and Jill make it up the hill? Or will it all come ... *Tumbling After?*

NARRATION SCRIPTS

Narration might be for anything from a story to an instructional manual. Below is just a little sample of this growing area of voice work. Try your hand at reading a book-on-tape or reading more cut-and-dried medical or legal text for further practice.

Children's Book/Story

The Little Girl Who Grew Up To Be A Snowman, by Yuri Lowenthal

"Oh, honey," he blurted. "I can't let myself get side-tracked by that business. My brain's overheating on this project as is."

And with that, he pulled a chain that tripped a switch that activated a mechanism that fired a spark that started a pump that compressed some air that sprayed his head with liquid nitrogen with a terrifying hissing sound.

"Ahh, that's much better. I'm close! I'm close!"

Classic Literature

Hone your skills on a classic; try something out of Dickens or Homer's *The Odyssey* for a little classical language practice. You can even use a play by Shakespeare or perhaps Molière. Pick whatever sounds like it might be fun. There's plenty to choose from. If you try something and don't like it, grab something else. Take advantage of free books at the library! For now, try reading the Aesop's fable below.

The Prophet, an Aesop's fable, translated by George Fyler Townsend

A Wizard, sitting in the marketplace, was telling the fortunes of the passersby when a person ran up in great haste, and announced to him that the doors of his house had been broken open and that all his goods were being stolen. He sighed heavily and hastened away as fast as he could run. A neighbor saw him running and said, "Oh! You fellow there! You say you can foretell the fortunes of others; how is it you did not foresee your own?"

Instructional

How to build a tasty PB 'n' J

First gather your ingredients. Lay out two fresh slices of bread (toasted if you prefer). Using a butter knife, apply one thick, even coat of peanut butter to one of the slices. Wipe the knife clean, and use it to apply an evenly matched coat of your favorite jelly to the other slice of bread. Carefully pick up the peanut buttered slice and turn it onto the jellied side of the other slice, so that the peanut butter is directly against the jelly. Press gently together. Voila! An American classic!

Legal/Medical

There are thirty-one pairs of peripheral spinal nerves which emerge from the spinal cord through spaces between the vertebrae. Each of these nerves divides and then subdivides into smaller branches. There are dorsal and ventral branches. The dorsal branches service the rear area of the body, while the ventral branches service the sides and front.

All rights reserved. Without limit to the rights copyright reserved above, no part of the publication may be reproduced without prior written permission of both the copyright owner and the publisher. Published in the United States, © 2009

Has all this copy inspired you to do some more digging of your own? Great. Anything you can read can be turned into practice copy. Take a look around and see what you might use as inspiration. The materials you compile will help you write commercial, narration, or even promo copy for your own demo!

Writing: Not So Solitary an Endeavor after All

I have had to sit in a studio watching some irritating former child-star ruin one of my best-ever scripts.

"My character wouldn't say that," she said.

"It's not *your* character," I replied. "It's mine. Now read the line the way I wrote it!"

Shortly afterwards, I was asked to leave. The writer is king in his little head, for as long as he is typing alone. Once the script reaches the studio, it belongs to the actors. Get used to it. Over the years I have learned to write scripts that are more open to interpretation, that allow the actors freer rein. I suppose it's because I trust them more now. I understand that on the day they have my script, it is theirs, and that I should credit them with the talent to do it justice.

The joys outweigh the miseries. I have listened as an actress took something I had written and utterly transformed it, adding nuances of her own, reading every line just as I had intended, but then adding tiny moments of unexpected comedy, pathos, and character. She took it to new heights, and she made it indubitably her own. Her name was Sheridan Smith, and she made me sound a lot smarter than I really was.

Those memorable little snickers from Mark Gatiss when he plays the Master in my *Doctor Who Unbound: Sympathy for the Devil*? They weren't scripted; he put them in himself. That filthy Scottish slang from Middenface McNulty in *Strontium Dog: Down to Earth*, largely invented by Mark McDonnell, who is a filthy Scot. That comedy snort from Johnny Alpha when he wakes up in *Strontium Dog; Fire from Heaven*, put in there by Simon Pegg, who is a comedy snorter. The decision to play the bad guy with the voice of Sean Connery in my translation of *Kekko Kamen* – all down to Rupert Degas. But don't tell anyone; I am happy to take the credit for their decisions, as long as I look good.

JONATHAN CLEMENTS, WRITER

A FUN EXERCISE: THE PHRASINATOR!

Scientists and technicians have been working around the clock at TaraYuri Industries and have finally devised a little something that we hope you'll enjoy: The Phrasinator (see below). Choose a phrase from the list on the left, and say it using each of the qualities (feelings) listed on the right. Be sure to try each phrase with each quality to discover how a different intention can change your reading of a line.

The Phrasinator can be a particularly helpful exercise for working on video game copy. If the director asks for two different takes of the same line, try giving a different intention, or quality, to each. Trust us; it'll be much more exciting than reading the copy twice exactly the same way. For the director *and* for you!

The Phrasinator

PHRASE	QUALITY
Watch out	Angry
Help me	Happy
I'm here	Frustrated
Not that way	Annoyed
What do you mean	Scared
I like green ones	Sleepy

I don't want any	In awe
Were you serious	Frightened
Get down	Excited
Yes and	Overjoyed
Hooray	Uncomfortable
That's what I'm talking about	Secretive

SCRATCH TRACKS   **WITH TARA & YURI**

CHAPTER 13
HINTS, TIPS, AND PARTING THOUGHTS

"Only those who dare to fail greatly can ever achieve greatly."
ROBERT FRANCIS KENNEDY, U.S. POLITICIAN
(SENATOR, ATTORNEY GENERAL)

We don't like to give *advice* per se, because everyone's experience is different, and advice implies that you think you know someone else's life better than he or she does. But these are things that *we've* done and they've worked for us. And not just for us, but for a lot of people we work with. So as we've said about the rest of the suggestions in this book, try one on, see how it works. If, after a while, it isn't quite right for you, change it, or move on to the next idea. There are plenty of tips to go 'round.

HOW TO STOCK YOUR PANTRY

All the actors we know have their own tricks and tips for keeping their voices healthy – because if you lose your voice, there's no real way around it.

Some of our favorite tools for soothing a sore throat or tired voice, or getting your voice prepped for an upcoming session, include all natural *black licorice, non-caffeinated hot tea, honey* (especially *Manuka honey,* an anti-bacterial, medicinal honey from New Zealand which you'll have to go to a health store to find), *primrose or fish oil* capsules, *lots of water, fresh pineapple* or *pineapple juice.*

Also, we eat a lot of *ginger* and *garlic* which are said to have natural antibiotic properties; and while that might not directly affect our voices, it seems to keep us healthy. Staying healthy is important because we've found that when we get sick, our voices are the first things to go. We've also found that *zinc* helps nip a cold in the bud, or at least loosen its grip on us. You may want to keep these things around so you'll have them when you need them.

You may find other things that are good for you. Great, add them to the list. Pay attention to what makes your voice feel good and what makes it feel bad.

Many people will tell you that before recording you should avoid *milk products* at all costs because it makes your voice thick and phlegmy, and in most instances they're right. But sometimes we actually like to have a little dairy if our voices are particularly scratchy or raw because it tends to coat our vocal cords a bit. Obviously (because we've said it so many times), drink as much water as you can without starting to feel sloshy. Not just before a session, but as often as possible. Staying hydrated will help a lot more than just your vocal health.

Black licorice (natural, not candy) is said to have anti-inflammatory properties which can soothe and slightly numb the vocal area, so it can be nice after a grueling session. But many people don't like the sharp taste. Yuri used to hate it, but after realizing how positively it affects his voice when it's scratchy, he's come not only to tolerate it, but maybe even like it. *Maybe*. Just a *little*.

Many types of *cough drops* can also be soothing. And while *lemon* and *menthol* (not necessarily together) are appreciated by some as a remedy, see how they affect you; some people actually find that the harsh properties of both lemon and menthol can aggravate a throat irritation.

Hot, *non-caffeinated tea* is nice for multiple reasons: it is warm, which keeps your voice loose and relaxed; and it keeps your throat moist. Honey, which can be mixed into tea or taken separately by the spoonful, has soothing and anti-bacterial properties.

Primrose or *fish oil* capsules, when ingested, are said to help strengthen your vocal cords and keep them lubricated. However, be sure to check the dosage: eating too many at a time could have … runny results. As with many types of natural *cures*, there is no scientific evidence proving that these oils will do something for the voice specifically, but the folks we know who use them seem pretty happy with their results.

Using fresh *pineapple* and pineapple juice as a natural anti-inflammatory is a tip that was given to us by a friend who has starred in many a Broadway musical. Singers often drink it or munch on it before, during, or after a show to keep the swelling in their vocal cords down when their voices are tired from overuse. Hey, good enough for Broadway is good enough for us; and besides, pineapple tastes good.

Some folks will tell you that besides *green apples* for combating smackiness, green apple-flavored hard candies or even a sip of soda will help. We prefer the apple since it's easier on the teeth and healthier in general. But once again, before you make your final selection, check with your body: it usually knows best.

Since you really just need the juice of the green apple, it's too bad they don't sell *green* apple juice. We'd buy it.

Things that we're pretty confident you should avoid to keep your voice as healthy as it can be are *smoke* and *caffeine*. Hey, like we said before, we're not your mom, your teacher, or the boss of you; but smoking and being around smoke seems like an obvious no-no, as smoke dries out your vocal cords and can change your voice, over time. Not to mention the effects of smoking on your lungs, mouth, etc. (we're sure you know this already). Once again, it is very much a personal choice. We know both highly successful voice actors who are regular smokers and highly successful voice actors who never smoke.

Caffeine has a very similar side-effect to smoke: drying out your voice and often creating more strain on it when you use it. So think twice before swigging that morning cuppa joe on the way to your VO session, tasty though it may be. Or at least consider decaf.

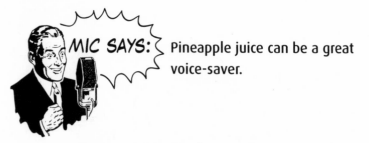

MIC SAYS: Pineapple juice can be a great voice-saver.

TARA & YURI'S SHORT LIST

Below is a short list of some of the things we think are most important. Hopefully, as you read through them, they will be a reminder of what you've read, and an inspiration for your journey. With everything you'll have going on all at once, it's always nice to have a little cheat sheet.

- **Agents**: Find a person (or more than one) that really *gets* you so you feel comfortable and confident with him/her/them as your go-between for job opportunities and clients. Don't just settle for whatever agent will take you.

- **Auditioning**: Remember the W's when looking at a script. It'll put you ahead of the game and help you stand out from the rest of the pack. Come up with a short ritual that will focus, relax, and ground you. Improv can help set you apart, but mind the script. Make strong choices, but be flexible enough to take direction.

- **Confidence**: If you can't hear what's going on in the control room, assume all's well. Make bold choices about the material and people will take notice. Don't feel you need to apologize if you're given direction to go another way; simply take it and move on. Don't ask the director if he or she needs another take, or if your last take was good: they'll let you know.

- **Creating Characters**: Playing with pitch, speed, and volume can be an easy way to find and develop a variety of different characters. But never underestimate the beauty of your own natural voice.

- **Demo**: Start with the voice closest to your natural speaking voice. That way, listeners will get *you* right away, even if they listen to only the first bit of your demo. When looking for commercial copy, feel free to flip through your favorite magazine and pull ads for real products. Then rewrite the material or tweak it to create your very own copy.

- **Efforts**: When it comes to efforts, just do it. But make sure you're breathing and supporting your voice.

- **Home Booth**: Home is where the heart is, but with a little effort and few bucks, it can also be a great place to record. The clothes hanging in your closet are a good substitute for expensive foam.

- **Hydrate**: Choose non-caffeinated beverages over drinks that have caffeine in them. Caffeine will dry out your vocal cords and not do you any favors in the booth. Water is best. Begin hydrating the night before to make sure you're well-lubricated come morning.

- **Imagination**: This is your most powerful weapon. Cultivate it and never underestimate it.

- **Location**: Go to where the work is. Your chances will always be better if potential employers can see your face.

- **Networking**: Use every opportunity to meet 'n greet as a way to build a network of people you can work with. You never know where your next job is going to come from, and most things are easier when you have other people to help you do them.

- **Popping**: Use your finger (or a pen or pencil) pressed into the *shhh* groove between your nose and your upper lip to help eliminate a plosive *pop* sound. Another great trick is to turn your head slightly off-axis (to the right or left) of the mic.

- **Professionalism**: Be on time. Be prepared. Be respectful. And just be a fun person to work with.

- **Read**: Read everything you can get your hands on. Read aloud. Read to yourself. Sir Ian McKellen once said that reading aloud is how he learned to act. Become better at reading and use this skill to your advantage.

- **Self-Promotion**: There are plenty of things you can do on your own to put yourself out there. Create a Web site, design postcards, carry business cards in your wallet, do a mailing. And that's just a start.

- **Warm up**: Warm up your face and tongue as well as your voice. This will help your voice resonate and create a warmer richer sound, as well as help prevent injury. So massage your face a little with your hands, loosen your jaw, and move your tongue around. You'll be surprised how much it helps. And how nice it feels.

In a Nutshell

Few understand that voice acting is *acting*, first and foremost. At the mic, there is nowhere to hide. Voice acting allows you to be ubiquitous and anonymous at the same time. Voice actors are like studio musicians – most are hired for their versatility, dependability, and because they bring a good energy to the studio. No one hires a résumé. They hire you because they want one less thing to worry about. My job is a service. My job is to provide producers something better than they thought they wanted.

Starting out in the big city, dig in, get a sustainable existence, and connect. Expect it to take years, not weeks or months. Every gig is ultimately an audition. Wanting to *break in* to voice-overs is like wanting to *break in* to being a professional athlete or the mayor of a city. Most who say they want it prove ultimately unwilling to earn it. Never take the meeting or hand in that demo *before* you are ready. You probably won't get a second chance. You must surround yourself with people going where you want to go, some hopefully a few steps ahead of you.

— Dee Bradley Baker, Actor

Resources

One resource we've found invaluable, especially for people just starting out in voice-over, is the *Voice Over Resource Guide*. This is available as a super-helpful and handy-dandy periodical guide as well as a Web site (*www.VoiceOverResourceGuide.com*)

with tons of great information. Here, you'll find info regarding classes, teachers, voice-over talent agencies, recording studios, union rates, demo reel producers, casting directors, and more. And the site is constantly being updated and expanded, so check back often.

We have no affiliation with the *Voice Over Resource Guide* Web site, nor are we endorsing any of the services advertised on it, but we recommend it because we've never found a better repository for this kind of knowledge. It can be a great jumping-off point to find a class, make a demo, or if you're already set in those areas, to research talent and casting agencies and do a mailing. We give this site *two mics up*!

Ross Reports and *Backstage Magazine* (*www.Backstage.com*) are two popular trade publications that also offer information on classes, agents, auditions, and voice-over related services. *Ross Reports* also periodically publishes special editions that focus on particular areas of the entertainment industry. In the *Voice-Over Edition* you will find detailed information on VO agents, the unions, and more. *Backstage* offers regional editions with more specific information related to local auditions. And by no means stop with these. A simple Internet search will turn up many more Web sites that provide information and resources related to voice-over.

For even more information, you might want to contact the unions that have jurisdiction over voice-over. As we mentioned before, in the U.S. those would be *SAG* (*www.SAG.org*) and *AFTRA* (*www.AFTRA.com*). You can find the closest chapters of these organizations as well as info on joining, dues, and much more on their respective Web sites. If you're outside of the U.S., find what union(s) help regulate voice-over work and ask them for more information.

You are, of course, always welcome to visit our personal Web sites (*www.YuriLowenthal.com* and *www.TaraPlatt.com*) and go to our *voice-over* pages. Here you can click on our different demo reels and listen to what we're using. Hopefully our demos will give you an idea of different types of spots, sounds, and qualities that might be helpful as you put your own materials together.

Also, our trusted friend and resource for all things audio and VO, Juan C. Bagnell, (who kindly contributed an anecdote to this book), maintains a helpful and entertaining blog (*http://someaudioguy.blogspot.com/*). Visit it at your own risk ... of *learning* something!

And your final resource: the Web site for this book (*www.VoiceOverVoiceActor.com*), which is filled with additional exercises and information.

As always, a wonderful resource is someone who is already doing what you want to do. Any voice actor that you know or have met will have his or her own story on how they got where they are today. Which brings us to our next section ...

STANDING ON THE SHOULDERS OF GIANTS...

A lot of our friends and people we work with on a regular basis are in the voice acting business. Some are actors, some directors, writers, engineers, agents, and more. We consider ourselves fortunate to work in a business with such talented, generous, amazing people who, by their sheer awesomeness, push us to step up to the next level and constantly improve our game.

Several of them had words to offer us, anecdotes or observations, that we thought might be helpful to include as we wrote our book. You probably noticed them sprinkled liberally throughout the chapters. We figured it'd be more interesting if occasionally you heard about the magical world of VO from people other than the two of us.

Here's what we want you to know about these people and why they're important to us: they're our family. You want to remember that you're going to build a family if you decide that you want voice acting (or any acting, for that matter) to be your life. The stronger your group is, the more you'll be able to accomplish, and the more fun it'll be. Be conscious of your growing family as you push towards your goal. As much as it'll sometimes seem as if you're all alone on your voyage, remember it's a team effort. So build a team you like, and they'll help you reach heights you never imagined possible.

MORE THAN JUST ENTERTAINMENT

I was a guest at Anime Next in NYC a few years back with a few other voice actors from *Fullmetal Alchemist*. In that series my character, Edward Elric, is a young boy with a metal arm and leg who seeks a mystical stone to restore his body and that of his younger brother. While we were signing autographs that Saturday afternoon, a young woman approached the table.

"I cannot tell you how much Edward has meant to me. He has gotten me through such a difficult time in my life and I feel like I identify with him so much."

As I listened to her, I wondered how she identified with Ed. She was probably in her twenties, seemingly healthy, and a girl. She started crying and said, "I don't care what my mom thinks, I want you to sign this." She stepped around the table to reveal that she had a prosthetic leg. She'd recently lost her leg in an accident and made such a connection with *FMA* that helped her through that difficult tragedy. We all proceeded to sign her artificial leg, not a dry eye around.

> From that point on, I realized that even though we are simply voicing animated characters, there are many people out there who draw great strength, encouragement, and support from our work. I came to learn that what we do has the potential to do much more than I ever thought before.
>
> VIC MIGNOGNA, ACTOR

AND *THAT'S A WRAP!*

Much like at the end of a recording session or on a film set, we're *wrapping* this book.

Or as a favorite director of ours likes to say in a thick Austrian accent, "Get out of the booth!"

We hope you've learned a bunch of interesting, exciting, and thought-provoking things during your read. And that you feel more prepared and more confident with the knowledge you now carry.

We wish you extra happiness and a second helping of luck in your many adventures. To move you toward your goals, take *daily* action – whether that's reading aloud, mimicking the radio, or training your body.

Also … don't forget to visit *www.VoiceOverVoiceActor.com* for more bonus goodies.

SCRATCH TRACKS **WITH TARA & YURI**

TARA! I FORGOT I HAD A SESSION TODAY AND JUST DRANK A MILKSHAKE!

AND A POT OF COFFEE! WHAT DO I DO?!

MAYBE THEY'LL ASK YOU TO PLAY "UNINTELLIGIBLE ALIEN #3".

OH, BOY.

DON'T WORRY ABOUT IT.

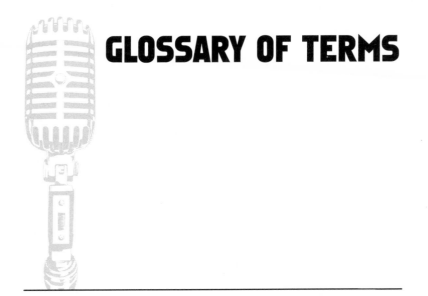

GLOSSARY OF TERMS

ABC take (series) – multiple takes of the same line in succession, usually to give the director variety

ADR (additional dialogue recording or *automated dialogue replacement)* – dialogue recorded to picture after something has been animated or filmed

AFTRA (American Federation of Television and Radio Artists) – a union covering many types of voice-over work

agent – a representative whose job it is to find and broker jobs for a client (the actor), and for which he or she typically receives a 10% commission

articulate/articulation - using the various moving parts of the mouth to create the vowels and consonants used in speech

bed – a continuous layer of background dialogue (*walla*) created by a loop group in post production to help create the illusion of a group of people; final audioscape may be composed of many beds layered together

beep(s) – a specifically timed sequence of audio cues (almost always three beeps) that, like a metronome, establish a rhythm and help the actor come in (start speaking) at the right time

booth – the room that you record in; a soundproofed space where the microphone and you create the magic of voice recording

callouts – shouts that you might record to break up a *bed* of background dialogue; created when you work in a loop group

cans – your headphone friends

clicking (smacking) - the mouth noises the mic picks up when your mouth becomes too dry; often makes a take unusable

copy – the dialogue you'll be recording; i.e. the stuff you need to say

demo – a brief recorded demonstration of your vocal talents; used as a calling card or introduction to a potential agent, manager, director, or producer

dialogue – spoken words between two or more characters

diaphragm – the muscular partition between the thorax (chest) and abdomen; facilitates breathing

diaphragmatic support – using your diaphragm to support and protect your voice when vocalizing

direction – the information which someone (usually the director) gives you to guide your performance

donut – group movement that involves the actors circling in front of the mic while conversing with others in the loop group to create a specific *bed* of background dialogue *dub/dubbed* – to rerecord dialogue translated from the original language or from temporary *scratch* tracks; also called *ADR*

efforts – the non-dialogue vocalizations you create to add life or action to a scene; sometimes called *reax* (reactions) or *onos* (onomatopoeias); usually grunts, groans, moans, or KI-yahs!

enunciate/enunciation – to create each sound clearly; to speak clearly

flap(s) (mouth/lip flap[s]) – the opening and closing motion of a character's mouth on screen

frames – the shortest increment into which a time code is broken down; each frame representing a still image of action which, when flashed rapidly in succession with other frames, creates the illusion of movement

free and clear – a direction used in group recording sessions indicating that the actors should not let their dialogue overlap

hitch – a slight pause that breaks up a line of dialogue

level – the volume at which you are speaking (engineers often ask for a level so they can accurately calibrate the recording equipment)

loop – a single line of dialogue (this term is a holdover from when recordings were done reel-to-reel and there was actually a loop of magnetic tape on to which audio was recorded)

loop group – a group of people (usually five to eight) hired to *loop* or record all the extra or *background* dialogue necessary in film, TV, or games; sometimes called a *walla group manager* – a personal representative hired to *manage* your career (for a 15% commission on all of your work) and help you make decisions that will advance you to the next level

mic – microphone; that thing you talk into

Mike – a common abbreviation of the name Michael (not to be confused with the aforementioned mic)

networking – broadening your circle of work contacts by going out to meet people in the hopes of creating new *mutually beneficial* relationships

node (vocal node) – a swelling on the vocal chords, often resulting from vocal strain; can affect the quality of your voice; an untreated node can become a nodule

nodule (vocal nodule) – a callus-like bump on the vocal chords; similar to a node; heals more slowly than a node and sometimes requires removal via surgery

nonunion – not belonging to a professional labor association that looks out for the welfare of its members (e.g. *AFTRA* and *SAG*)

notations (script notations) – specific details noted in the script that give you extra information regarding timing or visual cues; used especially with ADR/dubbing scripts

off-mic (off-axis) – turning your head slightly away from the mic so you don't *blow out* the levels when you have to scream, yell, whistle, blow …

OJ – original Japanese; the original Japanese animation voice recording from which an English dub is made *on tape* – sometimes said by the director or engineer to indicate that your next take will be recorded (a dated term that comes from a time when all recordings were made to magnetic tape rather than digital files)

original animation (pre-lay) – a recording of a character(s) that will be drawn and animated later specifically to match an actor's voice

passbys – movement that involves multiple people in conversation walking across the pick-up area of the mic to give the illusion of movement during a loop group session

phone patch – a telephone connection that allows the actor, the director, the producer, and/or the client to communicate during a recording session, even while physically in two or more locations (often with at least one participant in another city)

pick-up – the rerecording of a line because of a flub, rewrite, or a technical error, either during the original session or at a later date

pitch - the tonal placement of the voice as in high, medium, or low

plosive – the burst of air that comes with certain types of sounds, most notably the *p* and *b* sounds

Popper Stopper (specific brand name) – a metal or fabric mesh barrier that sits a few inches in front of the mic; used to cut down on p pops or other bursts of air that may distort the recording of sound; also sometimes called a *pop screen* or *pop filter*

popping (p pop) – the sound made when a violent burst of air rushes into the mic, distorting the sound; often created by a plosive

pre-lay – another way of referring to original animation recordings; laying down a recording before creating the animation

preview – viewing the moving image that you will be syncing to, before you record a take

promo – a voice-over recording commonly used to promote a network, show, film, or other special event

reactions (reax) – sounds that are used to color lines and give them a more realistic quality; similar to efforts but usually smaller

reel (demo) – a compilation of examples of your work, or demonstrations of your different characters or qualities

register – the range of an actor's voice, relating to pitch and placement (a high register tends to resonate in the head, while a lower register resonates in the chest and belly)

rolling (on tape, recording) – expression that indicates that the engineer is recording and that you're free to begin speaking

safety – refers to an *additional take*, recorded as a different option, or to be used if the original take is unusable due to a technical issue

SAG (Screen Actors Guild) – a performers' labor union typically known for its jurisdiction over motion pictures, but also governing some voice-over contracts

scratch tracks – temporary recorded tracks that act as a placeholder for dialogue to be recorded later; also, a side-splittingly funny 3-panel comic strip found in this book *script* – sometimes the lines you will be saying; sometimes the complete written story, including scene descriptions and every character's dialogue; usually seen as printed pages, but sometimes projected on a screen in the VO studio

script stand (stand) – a rack or other device on which you rest your script while you record

series (ABC take) – multiple takes of the same line in succession, usually to give the director variety

session – a scheduled period of time during which you record

sides – the partial script or copy that is made available to an actor for an audition; in the case of longer scripts, usually not the entire script

slate – an audio marker such as "Take 12" or "Tara Platt reading for Cinderella"; allows the engineer to identify a specific section of recording

smacking (clicking) - the mouth noises (clicking of the lips, cheeks, and tongue) picked up by the mic; caused by your mouth being too dry

sound check (level check) – a request from the engineer at the beginning of the session for you to read a few lines so that he or she can accurately gauge your volume

spec – directions included on your script to let you know what the client is looking for in your delivery of a character's lines

speed –how fast or slowly you speak your lines

splashy – a condition that occurs when your mouth is too wet and which causes unwanted mouth noise *spot* – another word referring to a commercial

studio – the location where voice-over is recorded as well as sometimes mixed; includes a recording booth and a control room

swag – promotional goodies that you give out (or receive!)

sweetening – adding additional sound (music, sound effects, additional dialogue tracks) to a VO performance to enhance it

sync – matching (synchronizing) recorded dialogue with mouth movements of on-screen characters

tag – a short bit of VO at the end of a commercial spot; identifies a certain product, or presents legal or other information regarding the product

take – one specific recorded performance of a line or series of lines, from the time the engineer begins recording to the time he or she stops recording; identified by a slate (*Take 1*, *Take 35B*, etc.)

talkback – system for the actor to communicate with director/ engineer while in the booth; usually means you (the actor) are hearing the others via a speaker in the booth; sometimes refers to communication over headphones

union – a professional labor association that looks out for the welfare of its members (e.g. *AFTRA* and *SAG*)

vocal attributes – your specific vocal qualities that create your unique sound

vocal cords (vocal folds) – the tiny flaps inside your voice box that press against each other to help create sounds as you push air out of your lungs *vocal creators* – the moving and non-moving parts of your face and mouth (lips, teeth, tongue, roof of the mouth) that help you articulate words

vocal node – a swelling on the vocal cords, often occurring as a result of vocal strain; can affect the quality of your voice; untreated, can become a nodule

vocal nodule – a callus-like bump on the vocal cords; similar to a node; more difficult to heal than a node, sometimes requiring removal via surgery

vocal signature (style) – your own unique collection of vocal attributes; like a vocal fingerprint, identifies you and sets you apart from others

voice match – the near perfect replication of one actor's voice by another

volume – basically, how loud you're speaking; sometimes how loud someone is speaking to you via your headphones or a speaker

walla - the background sounds that fill in a scene, sometimes made up of several layers of recordings to give the impression of multiple speakers

wild – to record without stopping to slate *the take* or otherwise give a marker identifying it; often occurs at the end of a session when trying to record options or anything that might be needed but hasn't been scripted

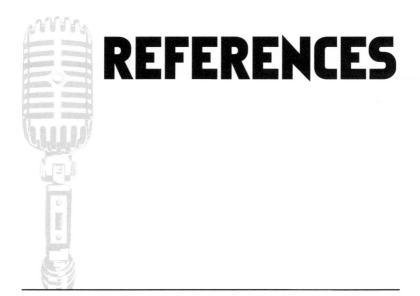

REFERENCES

"audio engineering." (2009). In *Some audio guy*. Retrieved July 13, 2009, from *http://someaudioguy.blogspot.com/*

Johnstone, K. (1992). *Impro: Improvisation and the theatre*. New York: Random House.

"luck." (2009). In *Merriam-Webster online dictionary*. Retrieved July 8, 2009, from *http://www.merriam-webster.com/dictionary/luck*

Mamet, D. (1997). *True and false*. New York: Pantheon Books.

Meisner, S. & Longwell, D. (1987). *Sanford Meisner on acting*. New York: Random House.

Parker, S. (2007). *Human body book, The*. (1st American ed.). New York: DK Publishing.

Parkin, K. (1994). *Ken Parkin's anthology of British tongue twisters*. London, UK: Samuel French.

"plosive." (2009). In *Webster's online dictionary*. Retrieved July 12, 2009, from *http://www.websters-online-dictionary.org/definition/plosive*

"radio." (2009). In *Wikipedia: Radio: history and commercialization of radio*. Retrieved July 8, 2009, from *http://en.wikipedia.org/wiki/Radio*

Rainford, N. (2002). *How to agent your agent*. Hollywood, CA: Lone Eagle Publishing Co.

"Simpsons, The." (2009). In *Wikipedia: The Simpsons*. Retrieved July 17, 2009, from *http://en.wikipedia.org/wiki The_simpsons*

Skinner, E. (1990). *Speak with Distinction*. New York: Applause.

Stanislavski, C. (1989). *An Actor Prepares*. New York: Routledge.

Townsend, G. F. (2009). In *The internet classics archive: Aesop's fables: the prophet*. Retrieved July 8, 2009, *from http://classics.mit.edu/Aesop/fab.3.3.html*

"voice-over." (2009). In *Merriam-Webster online dictionary*. Retrieved July 8, 2009, from *http://www.merriam-webster.com/dictionary/voice-over*

"voice-over." (2009). In *Wikipedia: voice-over*. Retrieved July 8, 2009, from *http://en.wikipedia.org/wiki/voice-over*

"War of the worlds, The." (2009). In *Wikipedia: The war of the worlds (radio)*. Retrieved July 17, 2009, from *http://en.wikipedia.org/wiki/The_War_of_the_Worlds_(radio)*

Yukelson, D. Ph.D. (2007). In Penn State University: *Teaching athletes visualization and mental imagery skills*. Retrieved July 13, 2009, from *http://www.mascsa.psu.edu/dave/Visualization-Handout.pdf*

INDEX

AUTHOR BIOS

Yuri Lowenthal, in addition to being a giant nerd, is an award-winning actor of stage, screen, and voice-over. He has worked on over 200 video game titles, but may be best known for his work in the popular *Prince of Persia* video game series, in which he plays the titular prince in *Prince of Persia: The Sands of Time*, and *Prince of Persia: The Two Thrones*. He's voiced Superman and Superman X on the Saturday morning animated Kid's WB show *Legion of Superheroes*, as well as Jinno/Kuma on the Emmy-nominated *Afro Samurai*. Catch him currently as Ben Tennyson on Cartoon Network's *Ben 10: Alien Force*, and as Bobby Drake, "Iceman," on NickToons in the animated series *Wolverine and the X-Men*. Anime fans may also know him from such series as *Naruto*, *RaveMaster*, *Kyo Kara Maoh*, *Gurren Lagann*, *Bleach*, *Code Geass*, and the film, *Robotech: The Shadow Chronicles*.

For additional credits, fun facts and information, please visit his Web site: *www.YuriLowenthal.com*.

Tara Platt is not a nerd but is proudly married to one. She has performed internationally from London to New York to Los Angeles in film, TV, animation, and theatre. In the VO world, she is best known for her work on the series and video games *Naruto* as Temari, *DC vs. MK* as Wonder Woman, and *Legion of Superheroes* as Dream  Girl. Anime fans may also recognize her from animated series and features such as *Digimon: Island of Lost Digimon*, *Buso Renkin*, *RaveMaster*, *FateStay-Night*, *Rozenmaiden*, *Tokko*, *Blue Dragon*, *Bleach*, *DearS*, *Boys Be*; and from video games including *Resident Evil: Umbrella Chronicles*, *Eternal Sonata*, *Soul Calibur*, *Final Fantasy*, *Desperate Housewives*, *Halo 2 (ilovebees)*, *Tales of Symphonia*, *Tales of the Abyss*, *Persona 3*, and *Valkyrie Profile: Silmeria*.

Tara and Yuri's production company Monkey Kingdom Productions recently finished their first feature film, *Tumbling After*. For more information on Tara or her credits, please visit her Web site: *www.TaraPlatt.com*.

bug bot press an independent
publishing company

QUICK ORDER FORM

Fax orders: 323.908.4101. Send this form
E-mail orders: orders@bugbotpress.com

- **Please send the following books or disks.** I understand that I may
return any of them for a full refund – for any reason, no questions asked.

Title   **Number of Copies**

_____   _____

_____   _____

_____   _____

_____   _____

_____   _____

- **Please send me more FREE information on:**

☐ Other books   ☐ Newsletter *(e-mail address is required)*

Name: _____

Address: _____

_____

City: _____ State: _____ Zip: _____

Telephone: _____

E-mail address: _____

Sales tax: Please add 9.25% for products shipped to California addresses.

Shipping by air:
  U.S. $4.00 for first book or disk and $2.00 for each additional product.
  International: $9.00 for first book or disk and $5.00 for each additional
  product (estimate).

Bug Bot Press
1335 N. La Brea #2233
Hollywood, CA 90028
wwwBugBotPress.com